MW01055608

The Colonial House Then and Now

1 (Frontispiece). *The Ogle House, a winter view.*

The Colonial House Then and Now

A PICTURE STUDY OF THE EARLY AMERICAN HOUSE ADAPTED TO MODERN LIVING

by

Francis H. Underwood

CHARLES E. TUTTLE COMPANY

Rutland, Vermont and Tokyo, Japan

Representatives

Continental Europe: BOXERBOOKS, INC., *Zurich*
British Isles: PRENTICE-HALL INTERNATIONAL, INC., *London*
Australasia: BOOK WISE (AUSTRALIA) PTY. LTD., *Sydney*
104-108 Sussex Street
Canada: HURTIG PUBLISHERS, *Edmonton*

Published by the Charles E. Tuttle Company, Inc.
of Rutland, Vermont & Tokyo, Japan
with editorial offices at
Suido 1-chome, 2-6, Bunkyo-ku, Tokyo

Library of Congress Catalog Card No. 75-28720
International Standard Book No. 0-8048 1150-4

First printing, 1977

Printed in Japan

Table of Contents

Part Two

Note: Stars (★) indicate old houses.

List of Illustrations

Note: With the exception of the Johnson and Dobyns houses, each of which was, for several years, the home of the author, all of the new houses are featured carrying the names of the original owners. The captions show the names of the present owners and the dates of construction. All of the houses are in Minnesota or Wisconsin.

Acknowledgments

The author's thanks are due to Warren Reynolds, who took the superb picture of the Johnson House on page 150, and to Downe Publishing, Inc., and "American Home Magazine" *for permission to use it; to the Society for the Preservation of New England Antiquities for permission to use the photograph of the Whipple House on page 44; and to William Newman, the author's old friend, who took the interior pictures.*

Author's Foreword

ALTHOUGH this book is primarily concerned with the presentation of contemporary Colonial houses, it seems only proper to use this foreword to pay brief tribute to the ancient dwellings that inspired their creation and from which they were adapted. The story of these old houses has been told often, and those readers who wish to pursue the subject further, after reading this book, need only turn to their public libraries, where they will find the fascinating tale presented with both words and pictures in many excellent volumes.

It would be presumptuous to think that one could add significantly to the wealth of material already available, but I do feel that the worth of this book is greatly enhanced by illustrations showing a picked group of the old houses along with the new ones. The photographs should be helpful to readers who are looking for ideas, and, at the very least, the inclusion of the older examples will provide the mellowed background against which the new houses will show up at their best.

The oldest survivor of the early houses was built only fifteen years after the first colonists arrived in Plymouth. It was English in appearance and utterly simple in execution, a fashion that was followed in most of the houses built for many years thereafter. Only the force of circumstance ever coerced early builders into originality or even into deviation from English precedent.

A new environment, of course, is fertile soil for evolution, so the passing of the years saw the development of simple new forms. When an increasing prosperity arrived with the dawn of a new century, an accelerated evolutionary process soon produced houses of great refinement. Indeed, their exhibition of good taste has not been bettered to this day.

More than 300 years have passed since the first of the New England houses made its appearance, and of those that were built during the following 150 years, hundreds are still standing. They are everywhere between Massachusetts Bay and the Connecticut River, and the attraction they hold for an increasing number of people shows no sign of abating. More and more people visit them each year, and each year more people are awakened to the fact that these old houses must, by any standard of comparison, be regarded as among the noblest that American architecture has produced.

These survivors from Colonial days range from the tiniest of cottages to houses of great size. They were built to last, and, fortunately for posterity, numerous historical societies and generous individuals are actively rescuing, restoring, and preserving many dwellings that have been unkindly dealt with by time.

When one sees such houses today on New England's country lanes and village streets, there is little to remind one of the hard and often fear-filled days of their early history. In their settings, now quiet and serene, they far transcend the ordinary. When the exceptional charm of so many of them is considered, there is no cause for wonder that such a great number of discriminating people, when they dream of a home, want something akin to those venerable dwellings for their own.

Appropriately enough, much of the material in this book was first put together beside a window looking out on Marblehead Harbor, Massachusetts, the picturesque New England scene in plate 2. For those who cannot make the New England pilgrimage in person, the camera provides an exciting substitute. It is here at hand; let us see what its perceptive eye reveals, in the introductory photographs (plates 3–11) and in the chapters that follow.

Publisher's Note: We regret the author's untimely death during the production of this book.

2\. . . . *from a window* . . . *The Harbor, Marblehead, Mass.*

3. . . . to this day . . . the many-chimneyed Hall Tavern (1760), Old Deerfield, Mass.

4. The Mashapaug House (18th century) looks very tiny, but . . .

5. . . . the view from the side tells a different story. Old Sturbridge Village, Mass.

6. . . . *transcending the ordinary . . . A classic New England cottage, Hansen, Mass.*

7. . . . *simple in execution . . . The Tristram Coffin House (1651), Newbury, Mass.*

8. . . . historic and inspiring . . . The Solomon Richardson House (1748), Old Sturbridge Village, Mass.

9, 10. . . . simple new forms . . . Colonial adaptations designed and built by the author.

A Chronological Analysis

of New England's Domestic Architecture from 1620 to 1800

OBVIOUSLY, no complete analysis of architecture can be encompassed on a page or two, and only the most sanguine individual would make such an attempt. But some sort of brief outline is a necessity for those whose knowledge of the subject is based almost entirely on misconceptions. It is in an effort to help clear up some of these misunderstandings that this summary is offered.

Unfortunately this is a topic whose component parts do not fall into precise slots. The evolution of the various types was gradual, but because it took place in different parts of the Colonies under different conditions, it was also erratic. The dates, therefore, are arbitrary. The subject is full of contradictions and surprises, and, actually, any of the types could have been built almost anywhere at any time. The reader without expert knowledge should keep these thoughts firmly in mind when reading the chart. There are two main periods:

1620–1780	The Colonial Period
1780–1820	The Federal Period

Broken down, these periods look something like this:

EARLY COLONIAL PERIOD

1620–36	Dugouts, wigwams, huts, and the first of the small permanent houses; of these none remains, but there may be seen, in both Salem and Plymouth, good replicas of these early shelters.

1636–1700 The medieval house: no paint; small casement windows with very small panes, usually diamond-shaped, set in lead. These houses were like the rural houses in England.

The cottage with chimney on one end, one room, and attic; or with center chimney, two rooms, and attic.

The two-story house with end chimney, two rooms, and attic; or with center chimney, four rooms, and attic.

The "salt-box" house, same as the two-story types with a lean-to shed added to the rear: cottages also often had these sheds.

During this period the gambrel roof became common on all types.

LATE COLONIAL PERIOD

1700–80 Prosperity increased in the Colonies. The double-hung window made its appearance, and the medieval house became a thing of the past. The evolution of the other types continued, and they became more refined. The axis of the roof of the two-story house moved from the center of the room below to the rear. There might now be eight rooms in the house and two chimneys, each chimney with four fireplaces.

THE FEDERAL PERIOD

1780–1820 The peerless McIntire (1757–1811) was now a young man in Salem. He built his bold, beautiful Peirce–Nichols house (1782). The splendid Federal mansions were in vogue. Charles Bullfinch (1763–1844), classically trained, returned from England in 1787, and the influence of the English Adam brothers was strong. New England architecture became great.

Shortly after 1700, Georgian design made its appearance. This design is usually divided into three phases: early, middle, and late. Because it was taken in its entirety from England, it should not be referred to as "Colonial." Its influence on the true Colonial types was so immense, however, that the two are often confused.

PART ONE

Our New England Heritage

The Homes of Our Forefathers

NOTE ON FLOOR-PLAN ABBREVIATIONS

Where possible, identifying information is spelled in full. The following abbreviations are also used:

G.—garage	L.—lavatory
K.—kitchen	B.—bath
Din. Rm.—dining room	H.—hall
Liv. Rm.—living room	C.—closet*
B. Rm.—bedroom	Sew. Rm.—sewing room
St.—study	Laund.—laundry
P.—porch	Dress. Rm.—dressing room
S.—shower	Stor.—storage
Eat.—dinette	

*Large, walk-in closets only are identified.
Measurements are given in feet.

THE VARIETY of forms from which contemporary Colonial designs are derived is almost without limit, and these ancient houses are often found in settings as enchanting as the structures themselves. Such a spot is Old Marblehead (plate 11). Virtually unspoiled, its narrow, crooked streets are lined with classic architectural relics of the years when the old Bay State was still a colony under the rule of a British king.

11. An enchanted setting, Old Marblehead, Mass.

PART ONE

The Cottages . . .

Of all the types of domestic architecture that have been developed in America, none has even remotely approached the popular appeal of the oldest one of all—the so-called Cape Cod cottage. It was from English counterparts that the first cottage developed, but there soon evolved the various American forms, of which many built in Colonial days still survive in New England's oldest towns. On these pages the three main cottage types, as differentiated by roof design, are to be seen.

12. A pitched-roof cottage, East Sandwich, Mass.

13. A gambrel-roof cottage, South Sudbury, Mass.

The pitched-roof cottage is the first type, illustrated by one of the jewels of Cape Cod (plate 12). Every detail of this East Sandwich house, with its many appendages, is a study in picturesque perfection. The Nobscot Cottage (plate 13), on the old Albany Post Road, shows the second type of cottage roof—the gambrel. The design of this house exhibits, too, a subtle disregard for symmetry that adds immeasurably to its charm. The third type of roof—a slightly bowed one—is seen on a venerable cottage built on Cape Cod's south shore. This grizzled veteran (plate 14) is an old favorite, recalling the hard early Colonial days.

14. A bow-roof cottage, East Falmouth, Mass.

The Gambrel Roofs . . .

Making general statements on early architecture is a risky procedure, but if one may be ventured at this time it is that the gambrel roof is the outstanding single characteristic contributed by New England to the domestic architecture of early America. As is evidenced by the Fairbanks House (plate 27), some of these gambrel roofs are very old. This is surprising in view of the fact that England did not seem to provide much precedent for them. Regardless of its origin, however, the use of the gambrel roof, once well started, spread with astonishing rapidity throughout the Colonies, and it was to be seen on buildings of every type and size. Well done, the gambrel roof is, aesthetically, most pleasing.

15. The Colonel Oliver Smith House (1761), Stonington, Conn.

The Oliver Smith House (plate 15) is a beautiful example of an old cottage whose perfect gambrel roof is crowned with a great chimney. Note the lean-to sheds on side and rear. They are used extensively on the new houses that we shall see later.

The Kendall-Holmes House (plate 16) is one of the oldest in Plymouth; sheltered beneath its ancient gambrel roof is an old ship's table that may have come from the Mayflower itself. The house was occupied by the same family for nine generations.

The Peter Toppan House (plate 17) well represents the two-story gambrel-roof house of the seventeenth century, although its present size was attained by putting two houses together.

16. The Kendall-Holmes House (1653), Plymouth, Mass.

17. The Dr. Peter Toppan House (1687), Old Newbury, Mass.

PART ONE

The Two-Story Houses . . .

During its transplantation from England, the architecture of the two-story house was less altered than was that of the cottage. The Parson Capen House, for example, might look more at home in East Anglia than it does in its delightful setting by Topsfield's spic-and-span common (plate 18). The house was constructed for Parson Capen's bride, a daughter of the prosperous Appleton family in Ipswich. When Parson Capen brought her to Topsfield she refused to live in the shack he had provided for her, and her father smoothed over an embarrassing situation by commissioning this handsome dwelling for the newlyweds. It is the finest surviving example of Elizabethan architecture. The best of the earliest two-story houses were built in this form. They contained four rooms, two on each floor, and an attic.

18. The Parson Capen House (1683), Topsfield, Mass.

19. The Manning Manse (1696), Billerica, Mass.

The Manning Manse (plate 19) and the Devereaux House (plate 20) briefly encompass the subsequent evolution of the English house in America. The Manning Manse is an example of the two-story house in its second phase, with the addition of a lean-to shed to the rear. This second phase became important in its own right when it developed into the salt-box house. The Devereaux House illustrates the third phase: the ridge now centers on eight rooms, four on each floor, and there are often two chimneys. Georgian embellishments appear more frequently as a result of increasing prosperity. Next door is the ubiquitous gambrel roof.

20. The Devereaux House (1727), Marblehead, Mass.

The Picturesque Salt-Boxes . . .

Many an old house started with a small nucleus; any future construction was usually a direct outgrowth of necessity. So when more room was needed in a four-room, two-story house, the easiest solution was to build a lean-to shed on the rear. These lean-to additions became very common. The resulting houses, with short roof pitches on the front and long ones on the rear, were called "salt-box" houses. The salt-box house then proceeded with its own evolutionary process, and what was born of necessity eventually became one of the outstanding architectural types in New England. More than that, it became, aesthetically, an outstanding success.

The three salt-box houses shown here are in Massachusetts and New

21. A salt-box house, Yarmouthport, Mass.

Hampshire. The first distinguished example of the type (plate 21) is in Yarmouthport, Cape Cod. The second (plate 22) is one of the varied salt-box houses that line the streets of Ipswich, Massachusetts. The old red house in the third photograph (plate 23) adds a striking note of color to the main street of Hancock, a more-than-typical New England village in the hills of southern New Hampshire.

22. A salt-box house, Ipswich, Mass.

23. A salt-box house, Hancock, N. H.

PART ONE

The Georgian Houses . . .

The Georgian style was New England's most distinguished architectural import. Developed in England to a state of near perfection, it was the style that had the greatest impact on Colonial houses. Although its sources were basically classical, its many forms and salient characteristics were easily adapted to the simple domestic architecture of the Colonies. The Dummer Mansion (plate 24) is an early Georgian structure in which the characteristic brick end with double chimney and parapet makes its appearance.

24. The Dummer Mansion (1715), Byfield, Mass.

25. The Pepperell House (1760), Kittery Point, Me.

Inspired by Georgian elegance, local builders were soon creating beautiful entrances and experimenting with pilasters, quoins, and modillioned and dentilled cornices. The Georgian style gave them the unlimited variety of Greek and Roman decorative forms that have ever since embellished the more modest Colonial types. The Pepperell House is a late Georgian mansion notable for its delicately carved brackets supporting the entrance cornice and its very fine projecting axial pediment with giant pilasters (plate 25).

After the Revolution, a simple form of Georgian house came into favor with prosperous but less-than-wealthy people. Many handsome dwellings resembling the Salem Towne House (plate 26) were built throughout the entire New England area.

26. *The Salem Towne House (1796), Old Sturbridge Village, Mass.*

The Oldest House . . .

The remarkable Fairbanks House (plates 27–29) is, for our purpose, an architectural document without peer. Beyond its weathered doorway lie the oldest surviving rooms of the English Colonies. The four additions to the original house, all completed by 1658, exhibit roofs of three different types; each one of these types later became characteristic of early New England domestic architecture.

In the Fairbanks House, the first part built was the center section, and it was, of course, strictly medieval in feeling, as were almost all the early New England structures of any size. The first addition (plate 28) was the lean-to shed on the rear (an integral feature, later, of the popular "salt-box" house). The gambrel-roof addition on the right was erected for John Fairbanks, the son of the original builder, Jonathan Fairbanks. The addition is complete in itself. If it was constructed immediately after John's marriage in 1641—and it probably was—its roof is very likely the oldest gambrel roof in America.

Another addition—to the parlor and a second-floor bedroom—is crowned with a hip roof; so is the entrance to John's quarters. The construction of a hip roof at so early a date was probably unusual; it would have been so much easier to build a shed roof. The hip roof also came into widespread use in the Georgian houses of the later Colonial Period.

It seems almost incredible that this oldest of all the surviving houses should embody so many of the characteristics that later became so common. But here it is to see—still standing on its original site, still framed with the original timbers brought all the way from England; although this frame has sagged in spots it is still absolutely sound and hard. The house, in fact, has never had to be restored and has never been inhabited by anyone outside the Fairbanks family. Substantially the same as it was left by its last occupant, Miss Rebecca, who lived there until 1903, it is presently owned by "the Fairbanks Family in America."

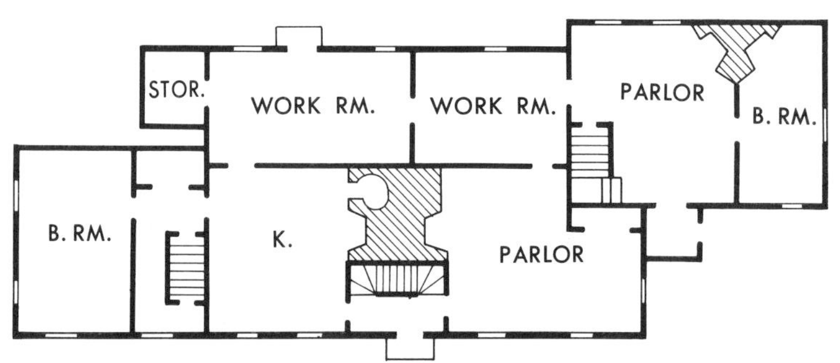

27. The Jonathan Fairbanks House (1636), Dedham, Mass.

28. Fairbanks House. Lean-to shed, rear.

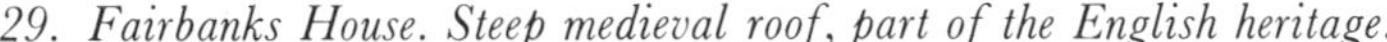

29. Fairbanks House. Steep medieval roof, part of the English heritage.

PART ONE

A Restored House . . .

From the low estate pictured in the old photograph (plate 30), the Whipple House, shabby and dilapidated from misuse, was rescued by the Ipswich Historical Society and restored to a semblance of its original appearance (plate 31).

The first part of the house's construction (the left side) was started by John Fawn about 1638. Not too long after this date the house was acquired by John Whipple who, during a period of years, made the

30. The Whipple House (1638), Ipswich, Mass., before restoration. Courtesy of the Society for the Preservation of New England Antiquities, Boston, Mass.

31. Whipple House, restored.

additions that brought the place to completion. For the next 200 years it was occupied by his descendants.

As an example of the early New England homes at their best, the interior of this great old house is unsurpassed. Furnished with the choicest pieces of that early period, it is now maintained as a museum.

As seen in the old photograph (plate 30), the original very small leaded-glass casements were at some time replaced with double-hung windows. The same thing has happened with all the very early houses still in existence. Actually, as mentioned in the chronological analysis (p. 22), the double-hung window did not make its appearance until sometime around 1700. In the early days, glass was a very scarce and highly taxed item, and there were actually instances when, according to a will, one heir would receive a house but the precious glass in it would be given to another.

The original site of the Whipple House was in what became a somewhat run-down section of the village near the railroad depot. It was, therefore, moved to a more suitable location by the south village green (plate 31). And there, serene in its restored dignity, it will remain as an enduring monument to America's past.

Museum of the Concord Antiquarian Society

This museum (plate 32) was built to house a memorable collection of antiques. It is a most exciting place, and within its walls a reasonably complete knowledge of the history and development of the interior architecture of New England can be acquired.

Shortly after the museum opened, the Perkins House (plate 33) was brought from Ipswich and connected to the rear of the new building. From the primitive rooms of this house the tours for visitors start. The tours proceed through fifteen notably authentic interiors and end on the third floor, where the great diorama of the fight by the old North Bridge is on display.

32. The Museum, Concord, Mass.

33. The Perkins House (1685), Concord, Mass.

PART TWO

Contemporary Colonial Houses and Their Old New England Prototypes

AS THE NEW houses on the following pages are considered, it will be seen that they have been carefully adapted from the old ones rather than authentically reproduced. An adaptation makes a better house for our time. There has been, however, no major deviation from architectural precedent, and in all cases an effort was made to capture and retain the character and charm of the old houses.

The smaller a Colonial house is, the more difficult it is to design, and in all our broad land the good ones are rare. A couple of the new houses on these pages are very small, and others are comparatively small. All of them are (as they must be) essentially simple. There is a paucity of ornamentation on their exteriors, and they need no more.

Within these serene exteriors may be created any form of inner charm that suits your fancy. The interior design and decoration may range from quaint provincialism to sophisticated elegance.

As for the floor plans shown for each house, they have an almost infinite flexibility. The things that can be done with extensions, with sheds and ells, and with lean-tos are limited only by the extent of the designer's imagination.

Readers looking for ideas are cautioned to remember that the great reservoir of inspiration is in the old houses themselves. Study them carefully—give more time to them than to the new ones. They have great adaptability, and a complete understanding of them is the first step toward the creation of a successful contemporary Colonial house. Generally speaking, contemporary Colonial design has become sadly mediocre. This unhappy state of affairs is the inevitable result of designers' copying from one another rather than turning to the original sources for their guidelines.

The houses illustrated here can be counted, we believe, among the few with sufficient character to satisfy the critical eye. But these pleasant houses, steeped in tradition, can speak for themselves. Their stories will be visual stories, and as you turn these pages you will find yourself embarked on a pleasant and, we hope, rewarding adventure.

PART TWO

The Judd House

In the Judd House (plates 34, 35), simple details, carefully worked out, give beauty and importance to what could have been a nondescript box. Within the 26 by 36 feet of this small house are three bedrooms, a good study, and two full baths.

34. The Judd House (1949). Owner: Miss C. M. Flemming.

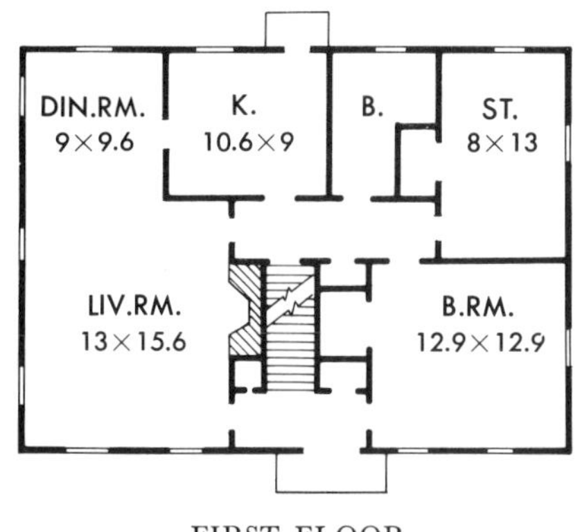

FIRST FLOOR

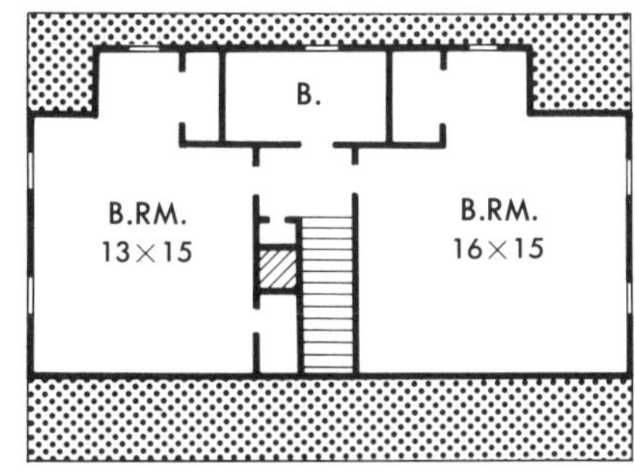

SECOND FLOOR

35. Judd House. Front view, showing dentilled cornice and shuttered doorway.

The Halverson House

The center section of the Halverson House (plate 36) is almost identical to the Judd House (plates 34, 35), but here each gable end has sprouted a wing, and there are also two front dormers. In such fashion can the contemporary cottage expand. Although this is still a small house the added length gives it a pleasantly impressive appearance.

We have here, too, an unusually good example of how important the seemingly insignificant details are. Consider the chimney carefully and you should have a feeling that there is something wrong with it. And there is something wrong: it has a top-heavy appearance. The house has just been painted, and the three projecting rows of brick (just above the white section) have been coated with black paint instead of white. When this small error is corrected, the appearance of the entire front of the house will be unbelievably bettered.

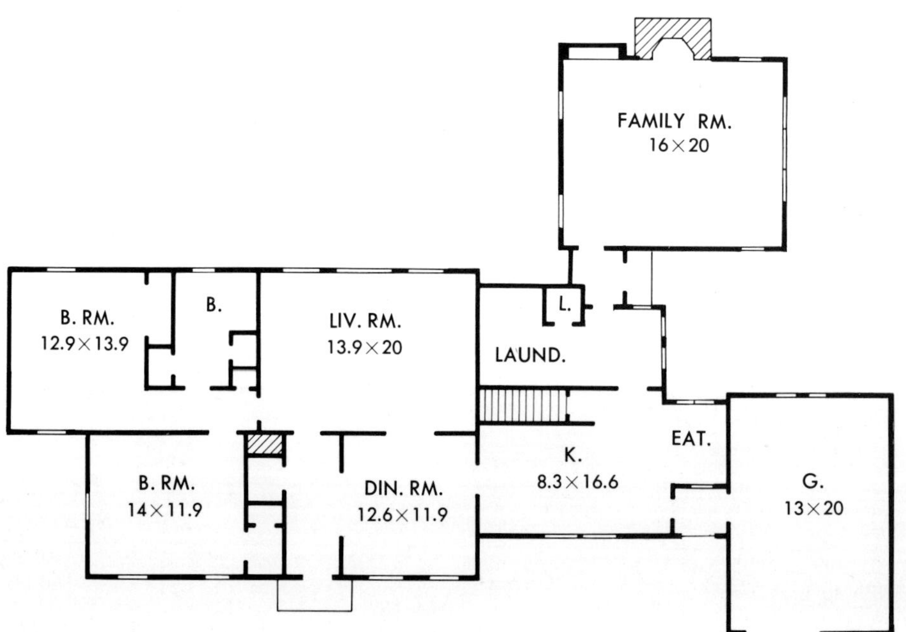

36. The Halverson House (1954). Owner: Mr. Archie Halverson.

The family room (plate 37) is an addition to the original structure. Houses of this type can take additions almost at random, and the invariable result is a more handsome and interesting appearance. With a slight change in the floor plan, the large attic could be put to good use. Move the partitions and chimney between the entrance hall and the front bedroom two feet to the left, and the hall will have room enough for a stairway to the second floor. Then, with the addition of a rear dormer, the present attic will have ample room for two good bedrooms and a bath.

37. Halverson House. The family room.

The Pease House

This is a freely adapted version of the early cottages, further proof that a small house need not lack either dignity or charm. The Pease House (plates, 38, 39) has both these attributes, to the extent of having once been featured in a national magazine as the "House of the Month."

The living and dining rooms of this house exhibit simply molded paneling (plates 40, 41).

38. The Pease House (1950). Owner: Mrs. W. H. Feldman.

39. *Pease House. Entrance.*

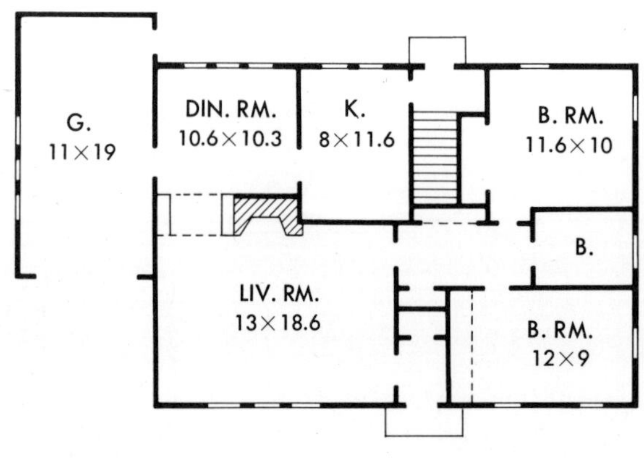

40. Pease House. Living room.

41. Pease House. Dining room seen from the living room.

PART TWO

The Ogle House

The Ogle House (plate 42) exhibits in simple form the enduring characteristics of the Cape Cod cottage. It could be the simplicity of these houses that strikes such a responsive chord in so many people.

The roof lines of the ells and appendages (plate 43) interlock beautifully and picturesquely, and, as usual, all of the parts are crowned with a chimney of massive proportions.

42. The Ogle House (1953). Owner: Mrs. K. V. Ogle.

43. Ogle House. Rear view, showing massive chimney and interlocking roof lines.

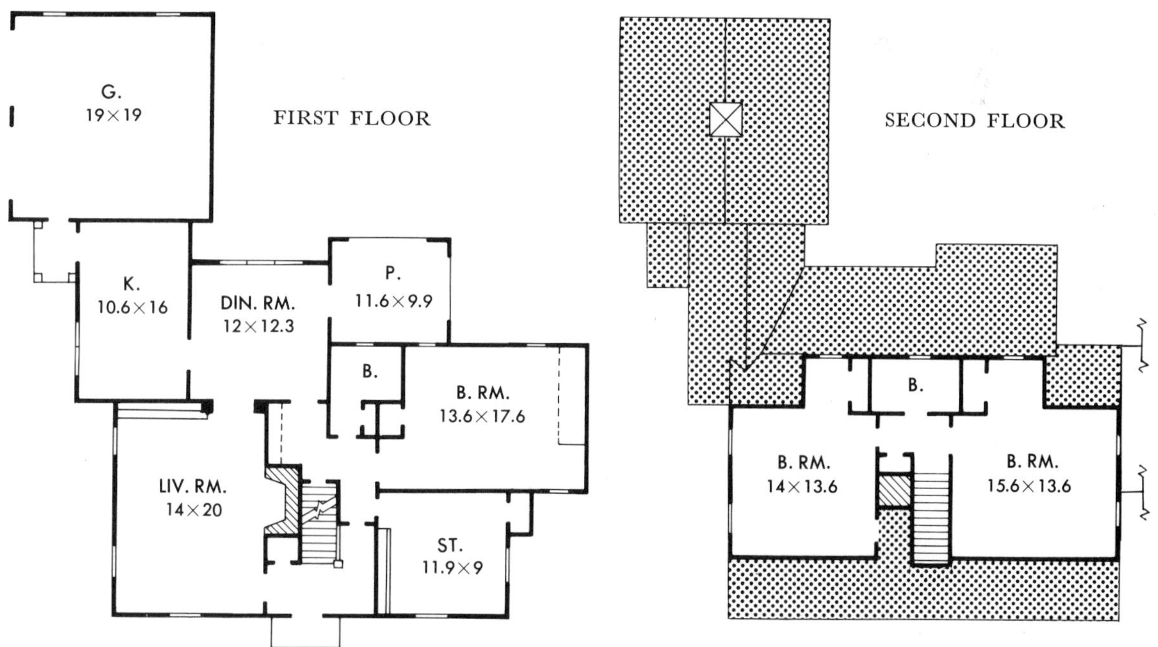

The Grace House

A gleaming white structure behind its rail fence, the Grace House (plate 44) is only minutes away from the home stadium where the Green Bay Packers have shredded the reputation of many an opponent. It is the home of one of the author's daughters, her husband, and their five children. A glance at the plan will show that it is a fine house for a family.

The Grace House's pleasing expanse of lawn (plate 45), once a deep and ragged gully, was reshaped into a beautiful setting. Even now a large city storm-sewer runs beneath the basement. This rear view gives one a better idea of the size of the house, which was purposely designed to look comparatively small when seen from the front. Actually, it stretches more than 100 feet from end to end.

As can be seen from the illustrations (plates 45, 46), it would be difficult to find a house with a more pleasing flow of roof lines. Those on most contemporary Colonial houses leave much to be desired.

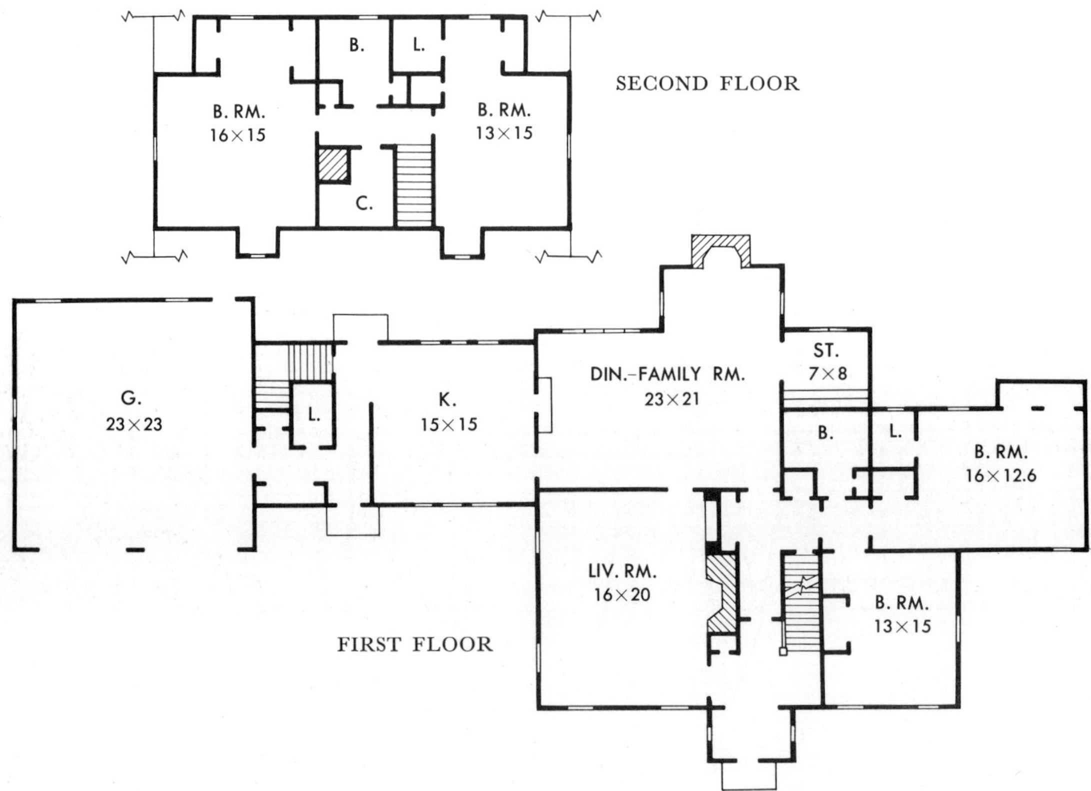

44. The Grace House (1963). Owner: Dr. J. B. Grace.

45. Grace House. Rear view.

46. Grace House. Rear view, showing roof lines.

The McKenzie House

The McKenzie House (plate 47) is reminiscent of those seen facing the sea on Cape Cod. Instead, however, it is on a plateau above the Mississippi in Minnesota. At this point the river widens to form beautiful Lake Pepin.

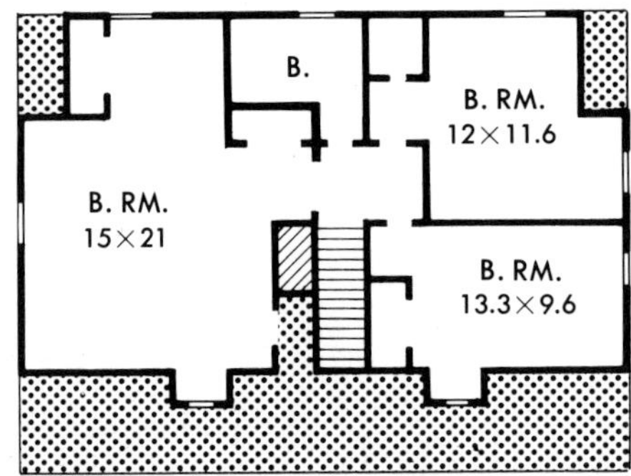

SECOND FLOOR

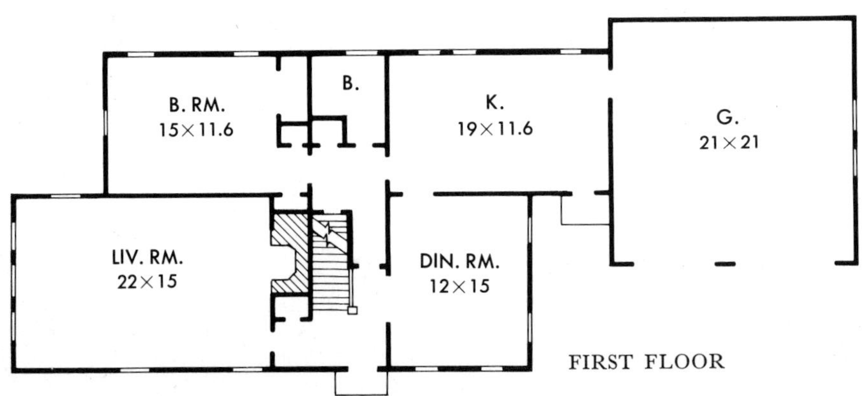

FIRST FLOOR

47. The McKenzie House (1956). Owner: Mr. David McKenzie.

PART TWO

★ *A New England Gambrel*

Many of the best gambrel-roof examples are on ells attached to larger houses. The architectural qualities of the ones on the Mulberry House (plate 48) are peerless. And added to architectural excellence is the charm of the eye-arresting chimneys that reveal a fine disregard for the usual form by pointing in every direction except up!

48. The Mulberry House (1752), Old Deerfield, Mass.

The Cooper House

If winter comes, no haven is quite so snug as a snug red house. And in all seasons lovers of Americana will be irresistibly attracted to the subtle charm of this red house (plates 49, 50) with its gambrel roof and its simple doorway sheltered by an ancient oak.

49. The Cooper House (1949). Front view. Owner: Dr. R. S. Rogers III.

The façade is aligned with a simple lean-to shed, creating an asymmetrically balanced effect, and the pilastered garage, with its hip roof, is unusual; it gives to the over-all picture a touch of unaffected elegance. Its white color, along with that of the lean-to shed, is in bright contrast to the red of the house (plates 50, 51).

50. Coöper House, with shed.

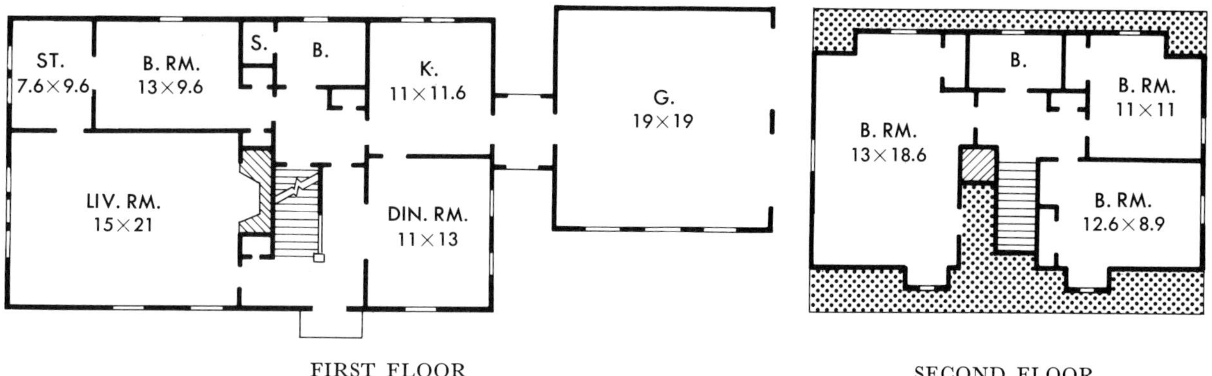

FIRST FLOOR

SECOND FLOOR

51. Cooper House, with garage.

PART TWO

★ *Small Gambrel-Roof Houses*

The gambrel roof is the author's favorite, and considerable space will be devoted to it on the following pages. It was tremendously popular in the Colonies, but it is an almost entirely neglected form today. This, indeed, is a mystery, even if only its practical contribution to second-floor space is considered. Without gambrel roofs, the second floors of these little houses (plates 52, 53) would have been almost worthless, and the Dyer House (plate 54) would have had two poor bedrooms instead of three good ones.

52, 53. Small gambrel-roof houses, Rockport, Mass.

The Dyer House

The sunny yellow Dyer House adds a pleasant note of color to its neighborhood. Too few homes are painted yellow today; no other color provides a finer background for green lawns and summer flowers (plate 54), and in winter it is the perfect foil for the tracery of naked branches (plate 55).

54. The Dyer House (1954). Owner: Dr. H. H. Young.

55. Dyer House. Winter view.

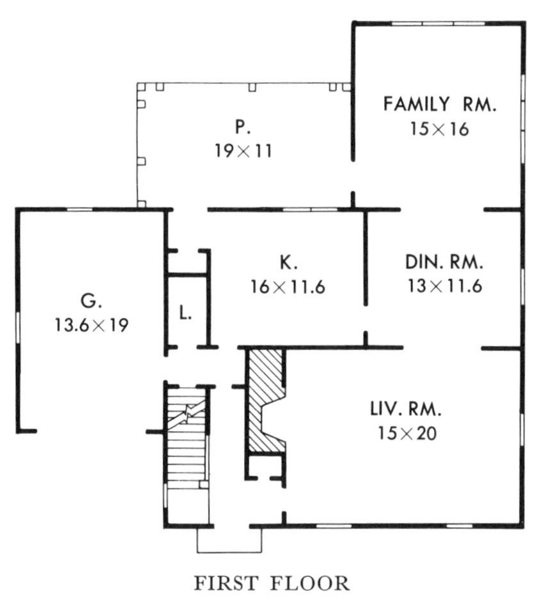

FIRST FLOOR

B.
B. RM.
13.6×15
B. RM.
16×10.6
B. RM.
11.3×20

SECOND FLOOR

PART TWO

★ *The Old Dwight-Barnard House*

Certain sights can never be forgotten, and the Dwight-Barnard House (plate 56) is one of them. Originally located in Springfield, Massachusetts, it was moved to a magnificent setting in Old Deerfield in 1954. Even at first glance, this old house is breathtaking, and to stand in contemplation before it is to experience the eerie feeling of being carried back to a long-gone century.

The component parts of the Dwight-Barnard House are worth close scrutiny. The Georgian influence is apparent, this time in the dormers of the main façade and in the entrance. Two of the dormers have low-pitched classical gables, and one is segmental. The entrance with its swan's-neck pediment is representative of the traditions of the Connecticut Valley at their best. These touches impart to the structure an air of solemn majesty; to the ancient street where it stands, the house brings nothing less than glory.

New England is a land of Gargantuan chimneys, and they usually strike the dominant note in pictorial composition. But, in studying the eye-catching details of the extraordinary ell structure on the Dwight-Barnard House, the monumental chimney passes almost unnoticed. As a matter of fact, this entire composition (plate 57) is rich in details that could be used to beautify and give interest to any house.

*56. The Dwight-Barnard House (*ca. *1754), Old Deerfield, Mass.*

57. Dwight-Barnard House. Ell structure with architectural details.

★ *Old Cottages: Entrances*

The traditional Cape Cod cottage is usually pictured, in the popular mind, with a center entrance. There were, of course, many variations from this form, and among these variations this house in Rockport, Massachusetts (plate 58) is one of the most distinguished. The chimneys, with their picturesque pots, are unusually slender, and the four windows beside a side-lighted entrance represent a wide departure from the ordinary. There is little limit, indeed, to the flexibility of the Cape Cod cottage.

58. An old New England cottage, Rockport, Mass.

The Ralston House

Shimmering in a sudden burst of sunlight, the Ralston House (plate 59) is bright against a cloud-swept, stormy sky.

We have seen that most—but not all—of the New England houses have center entrances. This house carries along the tradition of those whose doorways are to one side, with windows across the balance of the front. The floor plan was designed to take advantage of a river view.

59. The Ralston House (1954). Owner: Dr. D. E. Ralston.

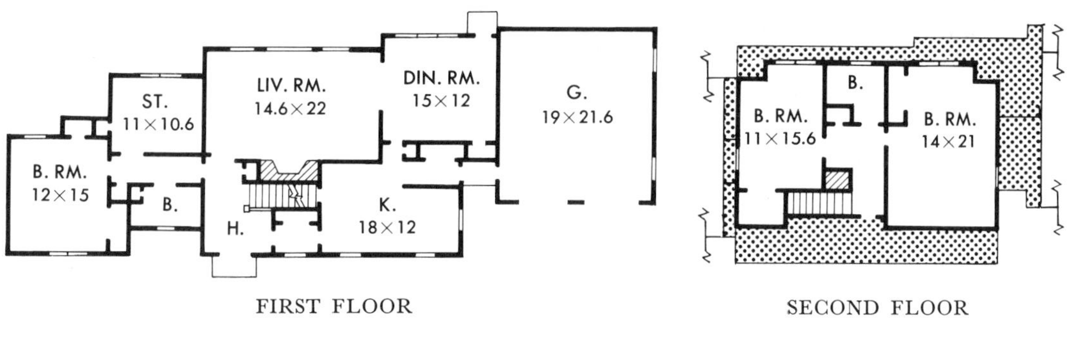

FIRST FLOOR

SECOND FLOOR

PART TWO

★ *Old Cottages: Proportions*

Massachusetts has a large share of classic Cape Cod cottages, while Connecticut abounds in unusual variations. These local tendencies can be seen in the unique proportions of one Connecticut gambrel roof and in the contrasting, classic form of a pitched-roof Massachusetts cottage (plates 60, 61).

60. Gambrel-roof cottage, Old Lyme, Conn.

61. Pitched-roof cottage, Duxbury, Mass.

The Blackburn House

This house is notable for its well-proportioned gambrel roof (plate 62), its inviting entrance (plate 63), and its beautifully finished and carpentered interiors (plate 64).

Although the first gambrel roofs were more picturesque than beautiful, they became increasingly refined (as did the other Colonial types). The sensitive design of the gambrel roof on the Blackburn House recalls these later examples, and these views (plates 62, 63) demonstrate the impressive dignity and beauty that can be achieved in a house of this type. The gambrel roof, although more costly to build than the pitched roof, greatly increases the size of the second-floor area (see plan).

62. The Blackburn House (1953). Summer view. Owner: Dr. W. W. Douglas.

63. Blackburn House. Front view, showing great chimney, 24-panel windows, and fluted pilasters flanking the entrance.

The study is an outstanding example of interior design, with its antiqued hand-rubbed finish, panelling, and furniture and its eagle-crowned bookcase (plate 64). The bookcase, built on the job by a master carpenter, is an adaptation of the Welsh dressers common in the Colonies.

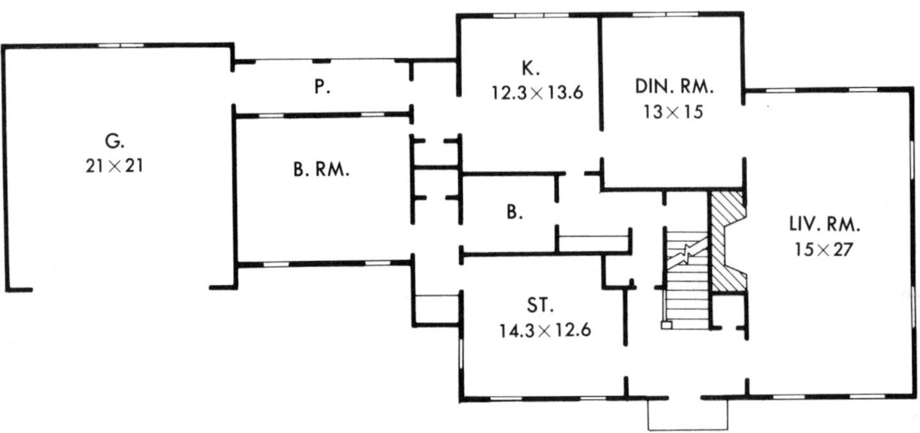

FIRST FLOOR

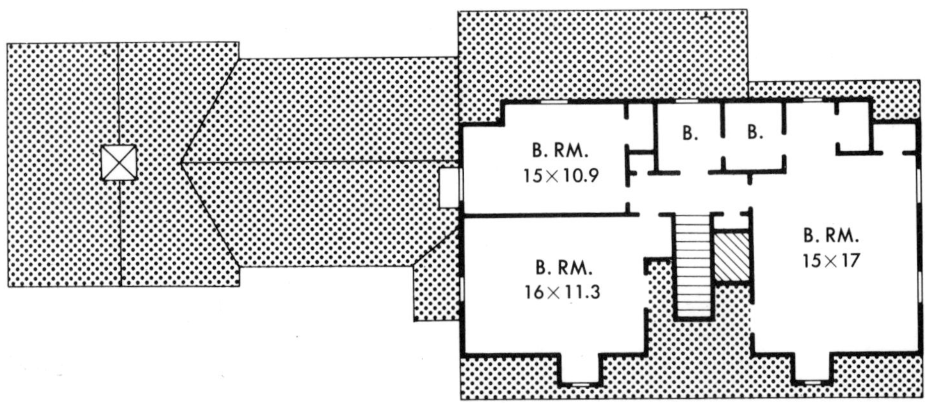

SECOND FLOOR

64. Blackburn House. Study, with eagle-crowned bookcase.

The Uihlein Cottage

The Uihlein Cottage (plate 65) is situated about a half-mile from the public road. After a drive through the woods, one comes upon it suddenly. In singularly attractive surroundings, with a broad expanse of water just beyond, the house in its setting is truly memorable. This cottage, although primarily designed for weekend use, is completely equipped and ready at a moment's notice for occupancy during any season. Windows fill almost all of one side of the large living room, from which one has a commanding view of a beautiful Wisconsin lake. The lake—cold, clear, and well stocked with fish—once suffered the indignity of being known as Sucker Lake, but the name it now bears is the more poetic-sounding "Wappogasset."

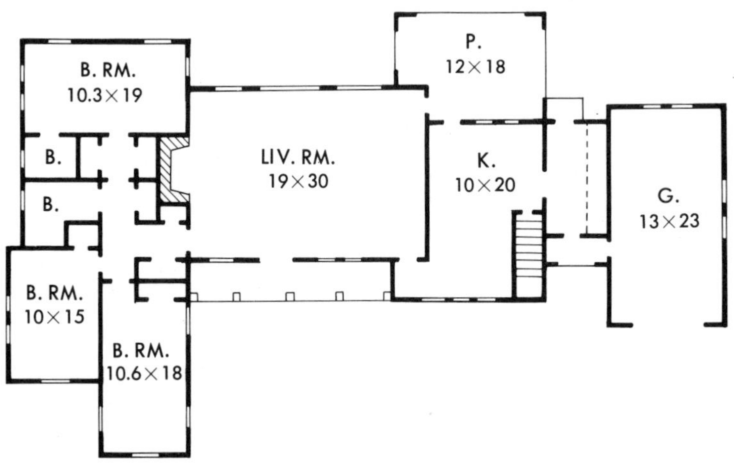

65. The Uihlein Cottage (1957). Owner: Mr. D. A. Erickson.

The Bush House

The Bush House, pictured here (plate 66) in the dull light of a Wisconsin winter afternoon, seems to consist of a small center section to which large wings have been added. In truth, it is no such thing. The roof pitch in front, to the left of the chimney, rises only part way and then becomes flat until it meets the pitch rising from the rear. The roof thus makes the part of the house that connects with the bedroom wing seem much shallower than the center section, when really they are both the same.

Little tricks of that kind can often produce excellent results. In this case an overwhelming expanse of roof was eliminated. Such a roof would have been a complete disaster. As the plan shows, the bedroom wing of this house is especially notable for its complete privacy and for the generous number and size of the closets.

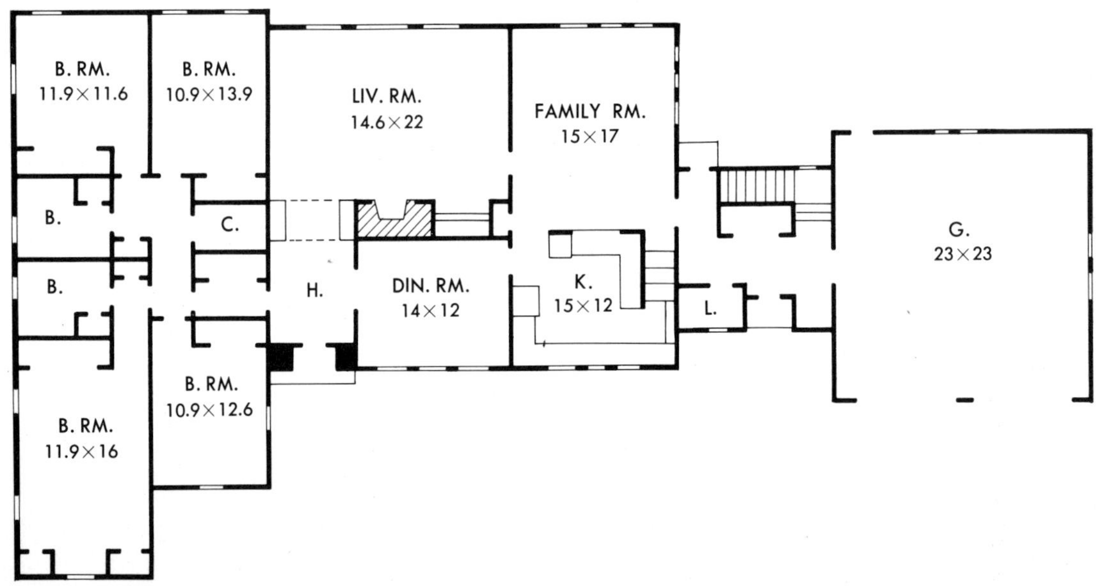

66. The Bush House (1960). Owner: Mr. Richard W. Bush.

The Spittel House

The cottage in its simple form is not easy to reproduce, and even the most competent designers often fail in their efforts. It needs a touch that is difficult to acquire; why so many early craftsmen could turn out such good ones is nothing less than a mystery. The charm of these craftsmen's old cottages defies description, and it is combined with a simplicity that is often utterly baffling. In reproduction, this simplicity perhaps presents the great hurdle, a hurdle that so often trips the unwary draftsman.

Today's rising costs, however, are creating conditions somewhat similar to those that existed in the early days. To do things simply is again becoming an economic necessity; higher prices will more and more dictate the use of simple forms, as in the Spittel House (plates 67–69). And, as this house shows, such forms can be used beautifully.

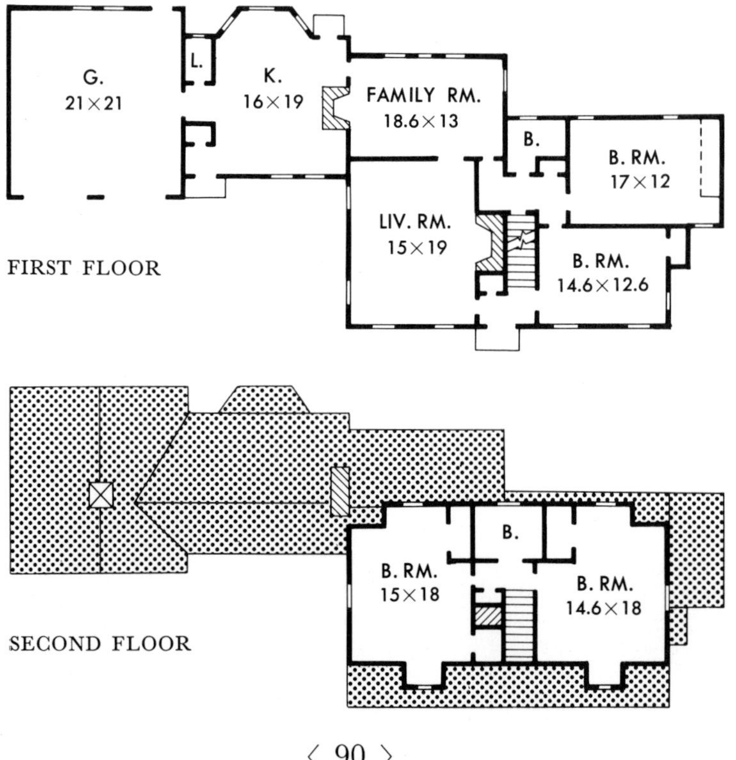

67. The Spittel House (1956). Summer view. Owner: Dr. J. A. Spittel.

68. Spittel House. Winter view.

69. Spittel House. Simple cornice.

PART TWO

★ *Two Old Houses: Levels, Windows, and Chimneys*

Proponents of the split-level house may think they have something new, but they are very much mistaken. The early split-level house shown here (plate 70) was built in 1640, only twenty years after the arrival of the Pilgrims, by Thomas Hart in Ipswich, Massachusetts. It was an unusually fine house for the period. In fact, some of its rooms were re-created, using the original woodwork, in New York's Metropolitan Museum of Art. (The woodwork in the original structure has been replaced by restorations.)

Another beautiful old house (plate 71) is situated only a few steps from Longfellow's Wayside Inn on the old Albany Post Road from Boston. The unusually striking appearance of this house is due to its interesting fenestration and also to the wild abandon with which it has grown additions and sprouted chimneys.

70. The Thomas Hart House (1640), Ipswich, Mass. An early split-level house.

71. House on the old Albany Post Road, near Longfellow's Wayside Inn.

PART TWO

The Dougherty House

Sheltered by towering oak and basswood trees, the Dougherty House (plates 72–75) gives the unmistakable New England touch to its enviable setting on the shore of a Minnesota lake. Its gambrel roof (plate 73) has a sturdy appearance never quite equalled in any other type; inspired by one of New England's favorite designs, examples like this one were built by the hundreds between Massachusetts Bay and the Berkshires, and are still being built there today. The subtly unsymmetrical façade (plate 74) lends interest to this contemporary house, which seems as much a part of the natural setting as the trees themselves.

72. The Dougherty House (1955). Owner: Mr. Thomas E. Dougherty.

73. Dougherty House. Gambrel roof.

74. Dougherty House. Façade view.

FIRST FLOOR

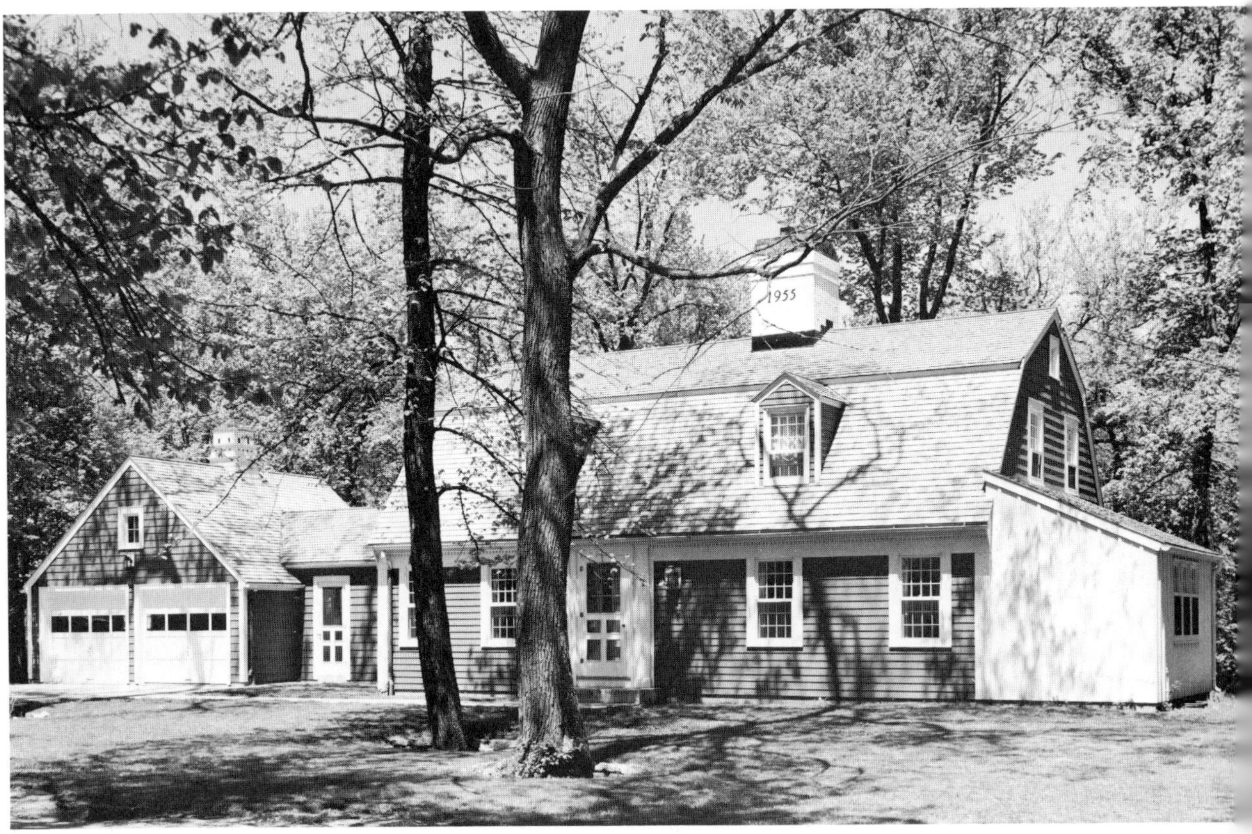

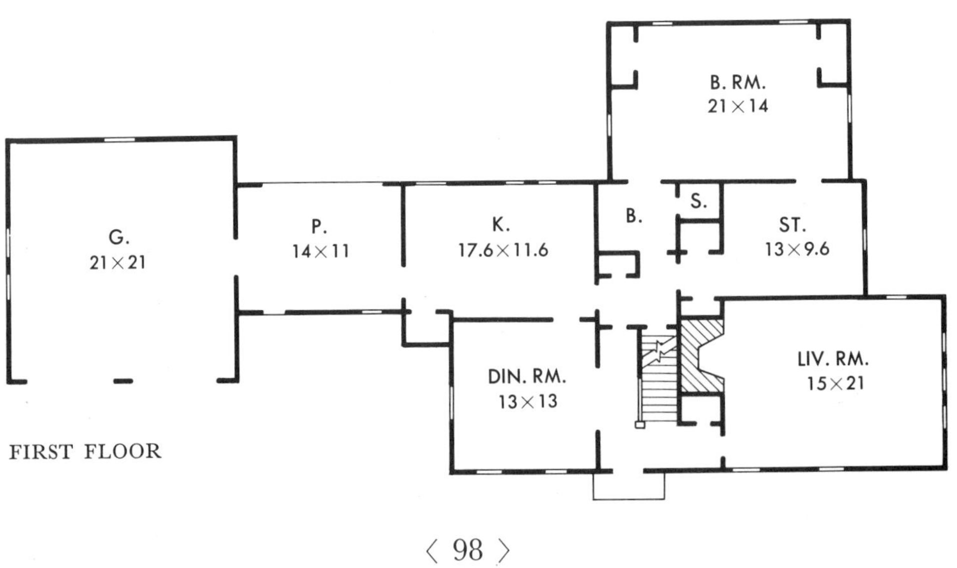

75. Dougherty House. Closer view, façade.

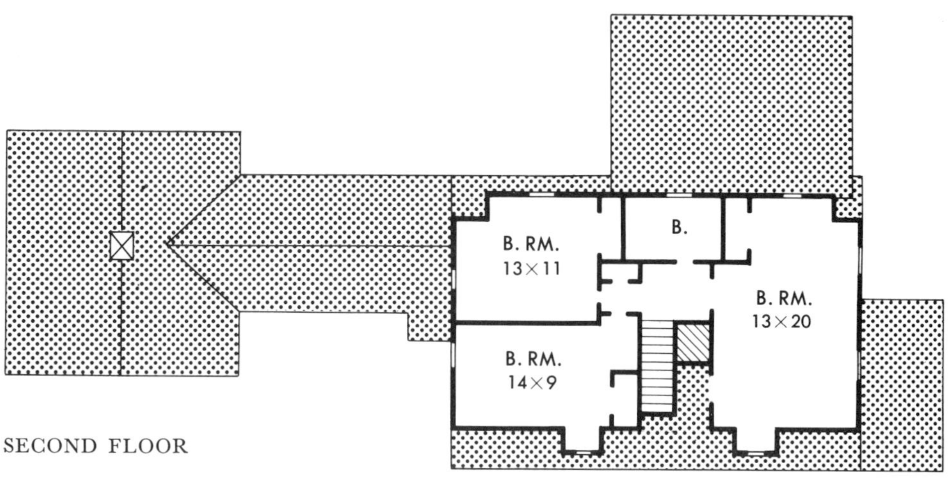

PART TWO

⋆ *The Frary House: An American Monument*

The oldest part of the Frary House (plates 76, 77) is the salt-box section, and it is one of the finest in all New England. Like the house with a gambrel roof, the salt-box design is a type that is almost entirely neglected today. And like the gambrel-roof house, its practical possibilities are almost unlimited. It is indeed peculiar that people today are so blind to possibilities that were obvious three centuries ago.

The Frary House is an American monument. Few old dwellings are as intensely exciting, architecturally, and fewer still have witnessed so many of the events of early American history. Only two houses survived the carnage and fire of the Deerfield massacre, and this Frary House is one of them.

76. The Frary House (1685). Old Deerfield, Mass.

77. *Frary House. Side view.*

Beneath the overwhelming elms on this ancient street there is a cathedral calm today, and one cannot view this weathered structure without feeling strangely moved. There is a sense of unreality; the present recedes into the past as one inevitably envisions the events of that dreadful February morning in 1704 when, led by Major Hertel de Rouville, 200 French soldiers and a band of 142 Abenaki and Caughnawaga Indians swept in from the morning darkness and enveloped the village. In the slaughter that followed, 48 Deerfield men, women, and children died, and 112 were taken as prisoners and marched off to Canada. During that fearful ordeal, 20 more met death.

An old burying ground is located a few steps west of this venerable house (plate 78), and there, beneath a mound, in a common grave, lie the remains of those who were killed that bitter winter morning. On the crest of this mound stands a simple stone, and on its side are cut these melancholy words: "The Dead of 1704."

The remains of Samson Frary, who built the first part of this noble house, lie beneath this austere marker. But where his wife lies, no one knows—for somewhere in the vast wilderness that stretched between ravaged Deerfield and Montreal she became one of those who were slain.

78. Marker commemorating Deerfield massacre of 1704.

★ *Two Historic Salt-Box Houses*

The first salt-box house shown here (plate 79) is in Quincy, Massachusetts; in it was born John Adams, the second president of the United States. Next door an almost exact replica of this house was built in 1663; it became the birthplace of another president, John Quincy Adams.

In 1940 the Solomon Richardson House (plate 80) was moved to Old Sturbridge Village, where it graces the village green, but it was built (believe it or not) in a town named Podunk.

These salt-box houses inspired the modern version shown on the following pages (plates 81–85).

79. Salt-box house, Quincy, Mass.

80. The Solomon Richardson House (1748), Old Sturbridge Village, Mass.

The Martin House

81. The Martin House (1954), Rochester, Minn. Owner: Mrs. W. J. Martin.

The Martin House (plates 81–85) was adapted from two New England salt-box structures (plates 79, 80). Like several other contemporary dwellings included in this volume, it is one unit in a grouping around a New England–type green. Designed with a careful regard for authenticity and perfectly adapted to modern living, the house makes an outstanding contribution to the appearance of the green as a whole.

The salt-box house has an ageless quality that has never been equalled by modern design and, as one might expect, there were many good reasons why this type was favored by the early settlers. It is practical and economical to build, and it is very livable. It can be large or small, plain or ornate, and it permits great flexibility in the layout of the rooms. This particular example is all house; within its 2,290 square feet of floor area are nine rooms and two full baths. The large chimney (plate 83) is a reassuring sight, though we are now kept warm by more modern methods.

The dining room (plates 84, 85) can be open to the kitchen—or a louvered door, swung up against the ceiling in plate 85, can be lowered to close off the area.

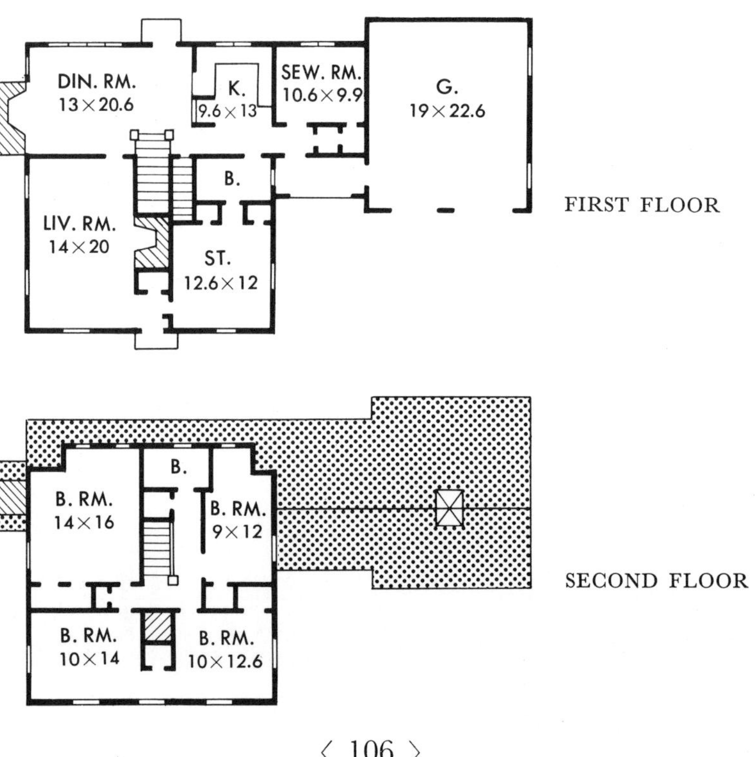

82. Martin House. Rear view.

83. Martin House. Closer view, showing large chimney.

84, 85. Martin House. Dining room, with view of kitchen.

PART TWO

The Edwards House

The Edwards House (plates 86, 87) is a true contemporary interpretation of the Cape Cod cottage in its traditional form. Its main section, like so many of those built in the early days, has a clapboard front and rear, with gable ends of shingles. The house is strikingly simple, and its attractive appearance is enhanced by its nice balance with the garage.

After these pictures were taken, a new addition to the right rear section of the house increased the size of the study by 50 per cent. This addition also provided a very large master bedroom with bath and spacious closets. And now there are fireplaces in both the bedroom and the study.

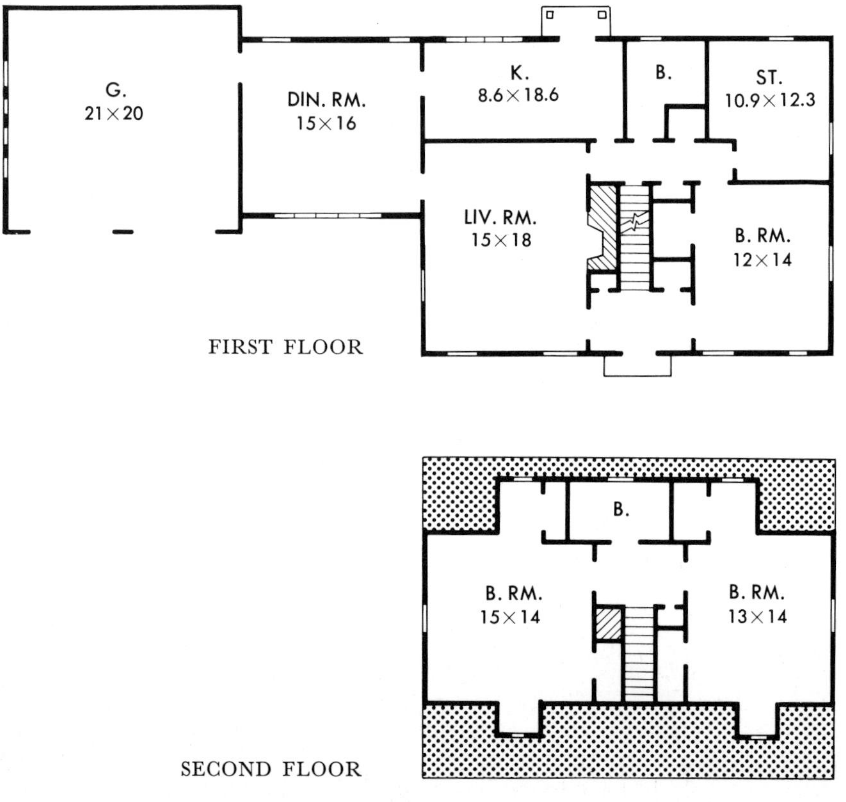

86. The Edwards House (1951). Owner: Dr. T. T. Schattenberg.

87. Edwards House. Garage view.

PART TWO

★ *Old Roofs and Dormers*

The Basset House (plate 88) was built in 1698 on the outskirts of Sandwich, the oldest village on Cape Cod. Its single dormer, above the door, is a rarity on the Cape and is, of course, an addition to the original house. All of the early houses were dormerless.

"The House with the Rainbow Roof" (its roof is slightly bowed) is known for its curious combination of roof lines (plate 89). It, too, is on the outskirts of Sandwich.

88. The Basset House (1698), Sandwich, Mass.

89. *"The House with the Rainbow Roof," East Sandwich, Mass.*

PART TWO

The Campbell House

The Campbell House (plate 90), with its many appendages, contains within its traditional exterior a finely detailed interior of considerable spaciousness. The exterior walls are a happy combination of boards and battens with shingles and clapboards. A view of the house, taken on a frigid winter day just after sunrise, shows two of the "additions" to good advantage and clearly demonstrates how a first-floor spaciousness is attained through their use.

The enclosed portico (plate 92) is used to advantage in this contemporary Colonial house. A glance at the floor plan below will show that it is the entry to a large center hall, and itself contains two coat closets.

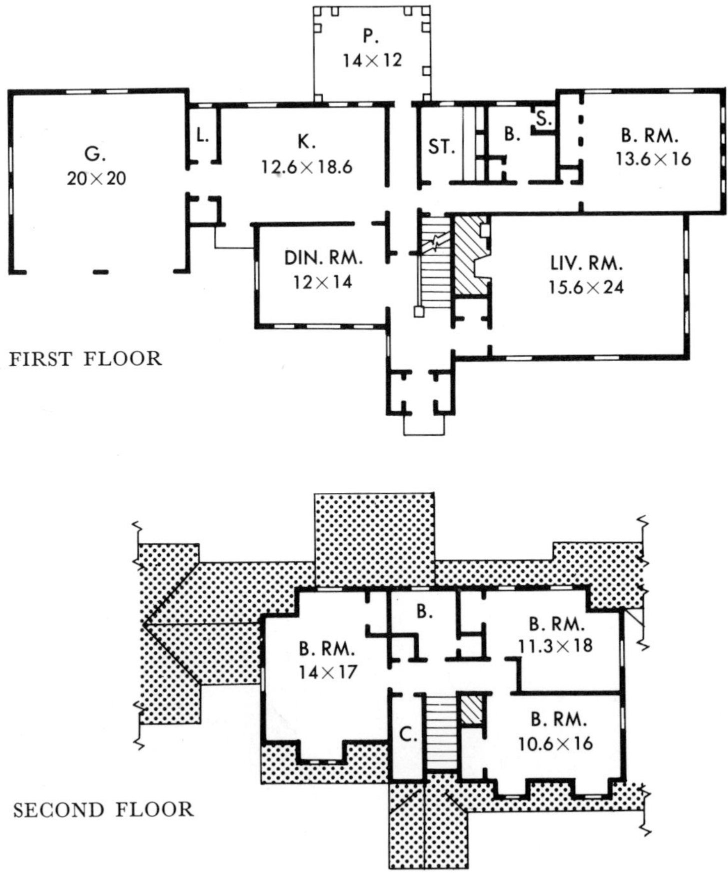

90. The Campbell House (1951). Owner: Dr. D. C. Campbell.

91. Campbell House. Two additions.

92. Campbell House. Enclosed portico.

The Underdahl House

Referred to as "Colonial," thousands of two-story houses have risen throughout the land and continue to proliferate like mushrooms. These houses too often are no more than clumsy boxes with holes in their sides for windows and doors. Only with the most diligent attention to the proportions of all parts of a house can one avoid such results. In the Underdahl House (plate 93), careful consideration of height, fenestration, cornices, and roof-pitch makes the difference between an ordinary design and a good one.

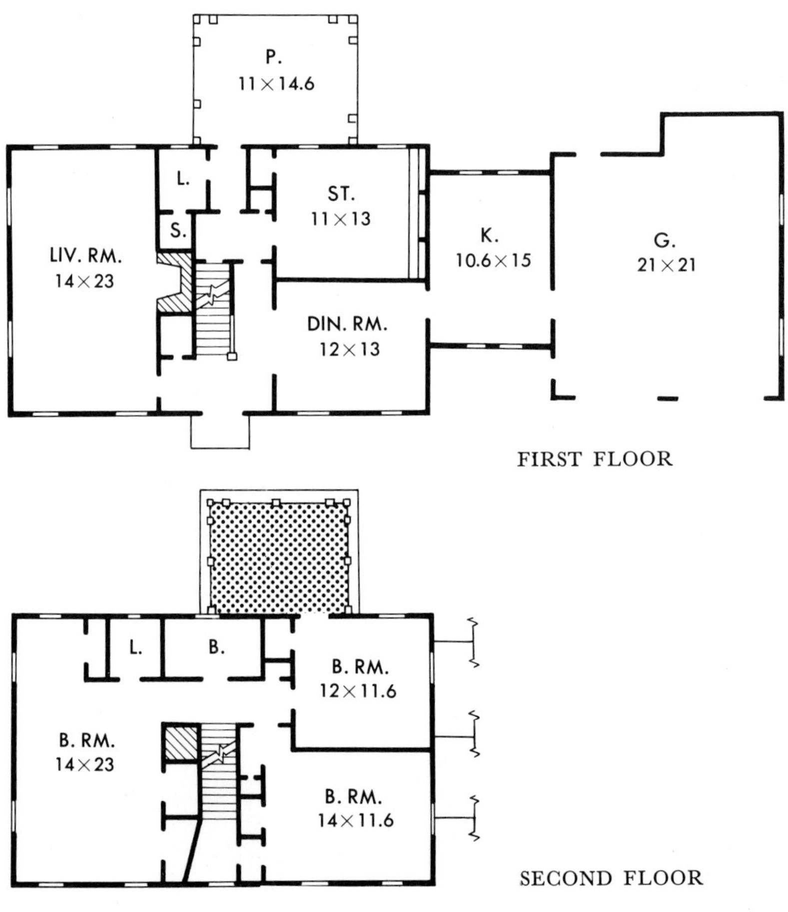

FIRST FLOOR

SECOND FLOOR

93. The Underdahl House (1950). Owner: Dr. L. O. Underdahl.

The hospitable entrance to this house (plate 94) is symbolic of restraint and dignity. Delicately carved and pilastered, it typifies the designs that appeared when more gracious houses began to supplant the unadorned examples of the seventeenth century.

94. Underdahl House. Carved, pilastered entrance.

The ReMine House

95. The ReMine House (1952). Gable end facing street. Owner: Dr. J. C. Hunt.

Although it follows no particular architectural precedent, the ReMine House (plate 95) is a popular one, with the unmistakable flavor of New England. The placing of the gable end toward the street was dictated by the shape of the lot, and it has proved effective. The great chimney, more reminiscent of Williamsburg, Virginia than of Cape Cod, added the final touch needed to transform what could have been an ordinary exterior into one that commands attention. A porch with flattened arches, a quaint dormer, and a tiny cupola (plate 96) are small details that combine to give this house character.

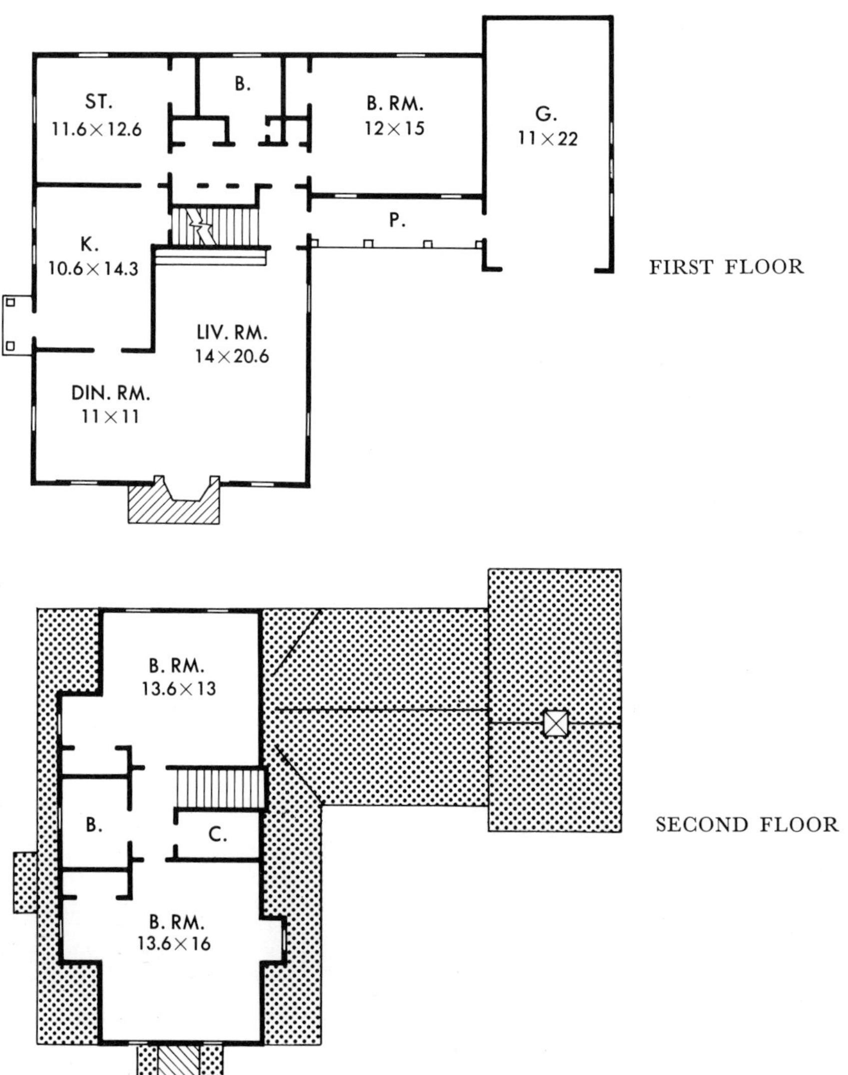

96. ReMine House. Porch view.

PART TWO

★ *A Connecticut Country House*

New England's best farmhouses are unequalled in the United States. Often huge in size, they have a dignity marvelous to behold. And what is a common sight throughout the countryside of those five New England states is a rarity elsewhere. Not all New England farmhouses, of course, have the unusually well-cared-for appearance of the handsome Enfield, Connecticut place shown here (plate 97). Many, nevertheless, show at a glance the great pride their owners take in them. And well they might—character is as integral a part of these structures as the beams and boards with which they were built and the pegs and nails that hold them together.

97. An imposing New England farmhouse, Enfield, Conn.

The Lipscomb House

98. The Lipscomb House (1951). Entrance. Owner: Dr. D. R. Sanderson.

A pleasant collaboration between architect F. Clare Hinckley and the author produced the Lipscomb House (plates 98–100).

Although this design represents a somewhat marked departure from the early forms, it could never be referred to as anything other than "Colonial." The house is built for country living, and is desirably located on a high hill; its sweeping view of the Zumbro River Valley in Minnesota extends for many miles. Its exterior is a pleasing combination of boards with battens, hand-split shingles, and white-painted brick. The interior layout is quite open, and the rooms are large and informal, with generous window areas.

This house will never become dated. It illustrates to perfection the ease with which the old forms and details adapt themselves to modern purposes.

99. Lipscomb House. Front view.

100. Lipscomb House. Rear view.

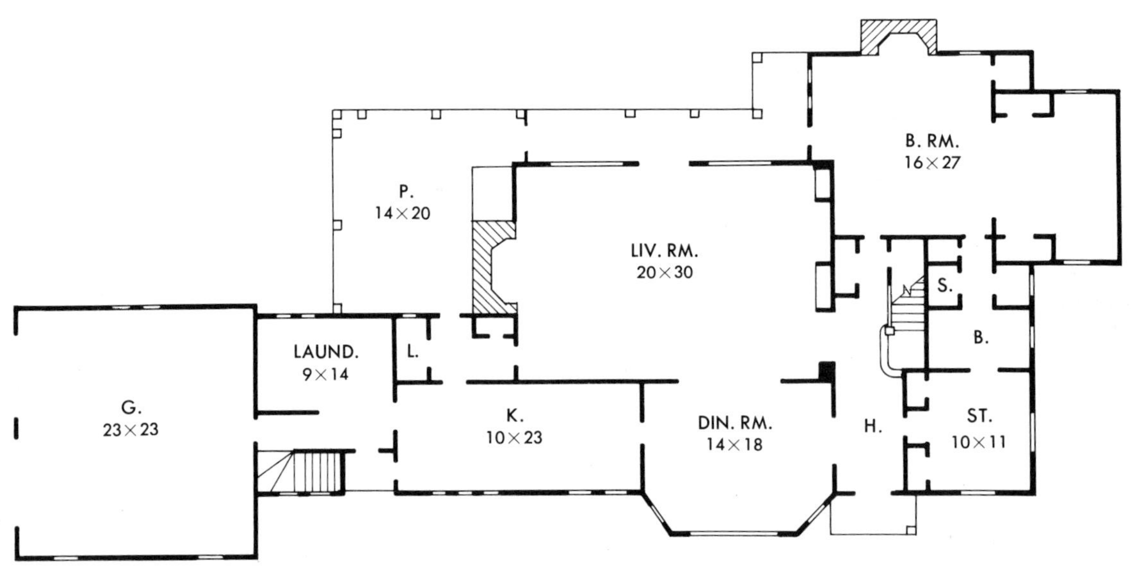

FIRST FLOOR

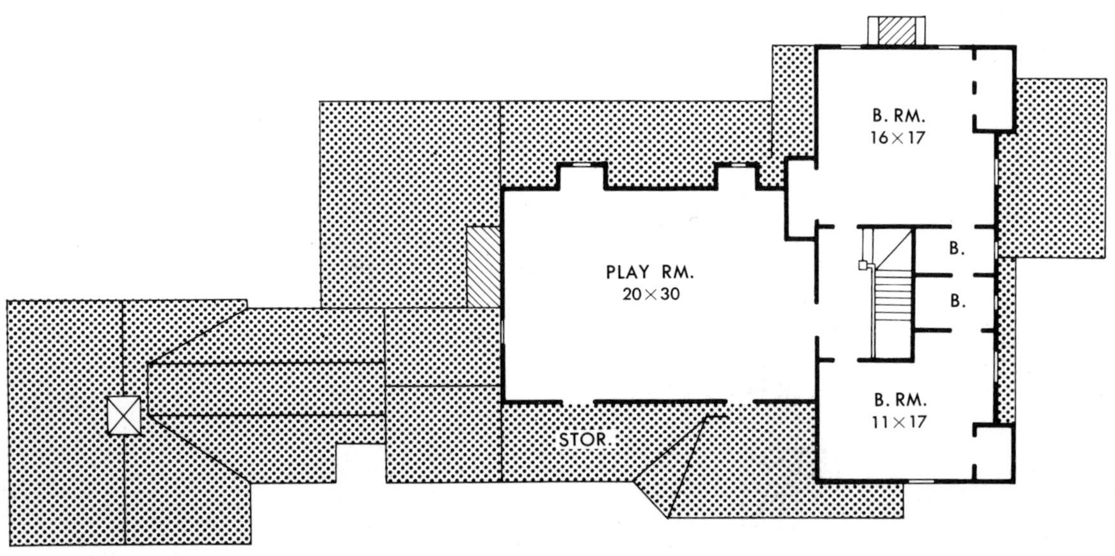

SECOND FLOOR

The Lawler House

101. The Lawler House (1953). Original structure on right. Owner: Dr. J. M. Stickney.

The architectural prototypes of the Lawler House (plates 101–103), were known as "half-houses," and they were exactly what the name suggests. In a house like this, the right side would have been the original structure, with the chimney at one end. Later, when necessity demanded or prosperity permitted, the other half would have been built. Sometimes, as in this house, it would be smaller, but usually it would duplicate the original half in depth and height and thus present the appearance of a cottage that had all been built at the same time.

The floor plan has a notable flexibility that permits its use in the creation of dwellings that have no similarity to this one. The floor plans of the Ogle, Grace, Spittel, and Dobyns houses (pp. 61, 62, 90, and 159) were adapted from this layout.

102. Lawler House. Rear view.

103. Lawler House. Side view, showing later additions.

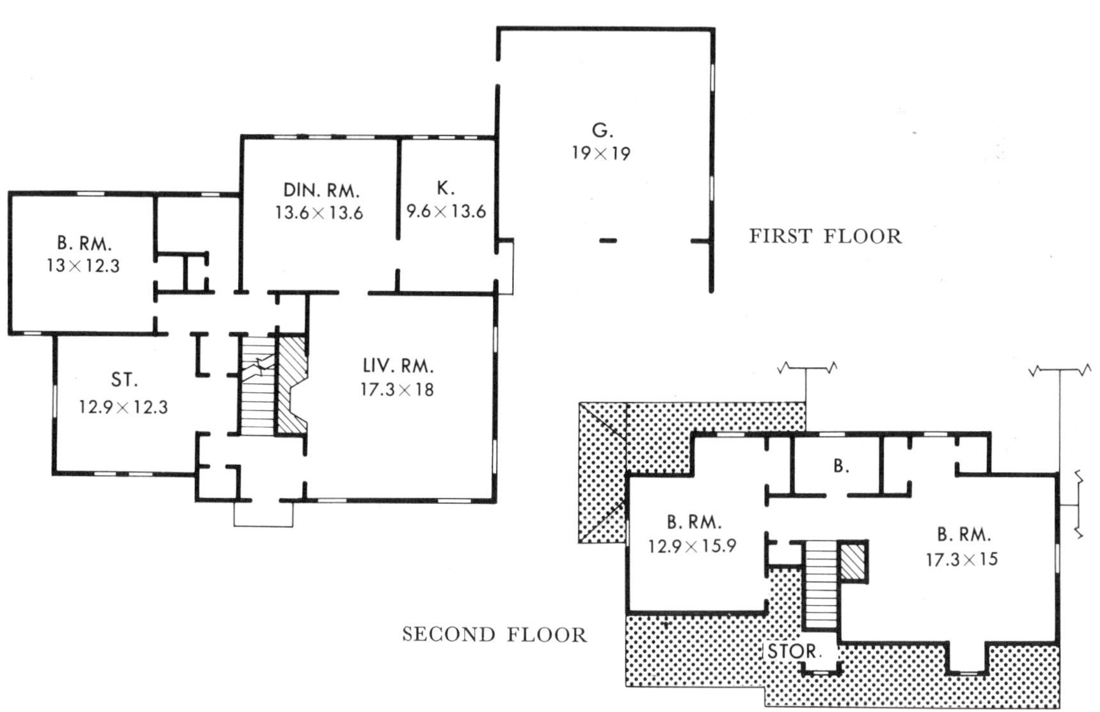

The Randall House

The Randall House (plate 104) displays its ancient heritage with an air of quiet dignity, a quality inherent in its predecessors and one too often lacking in contemporary design. The shed-roof dormers seen here were not commonly used on the pitched-roof cottage but they present a pleasing variation from the more familiar form.

There is no exact recipe for a good cottage, but among the various ingredients a plump chimney, a sheltered doorway, and an apple tree (plate 105) will prove to be very tasty.

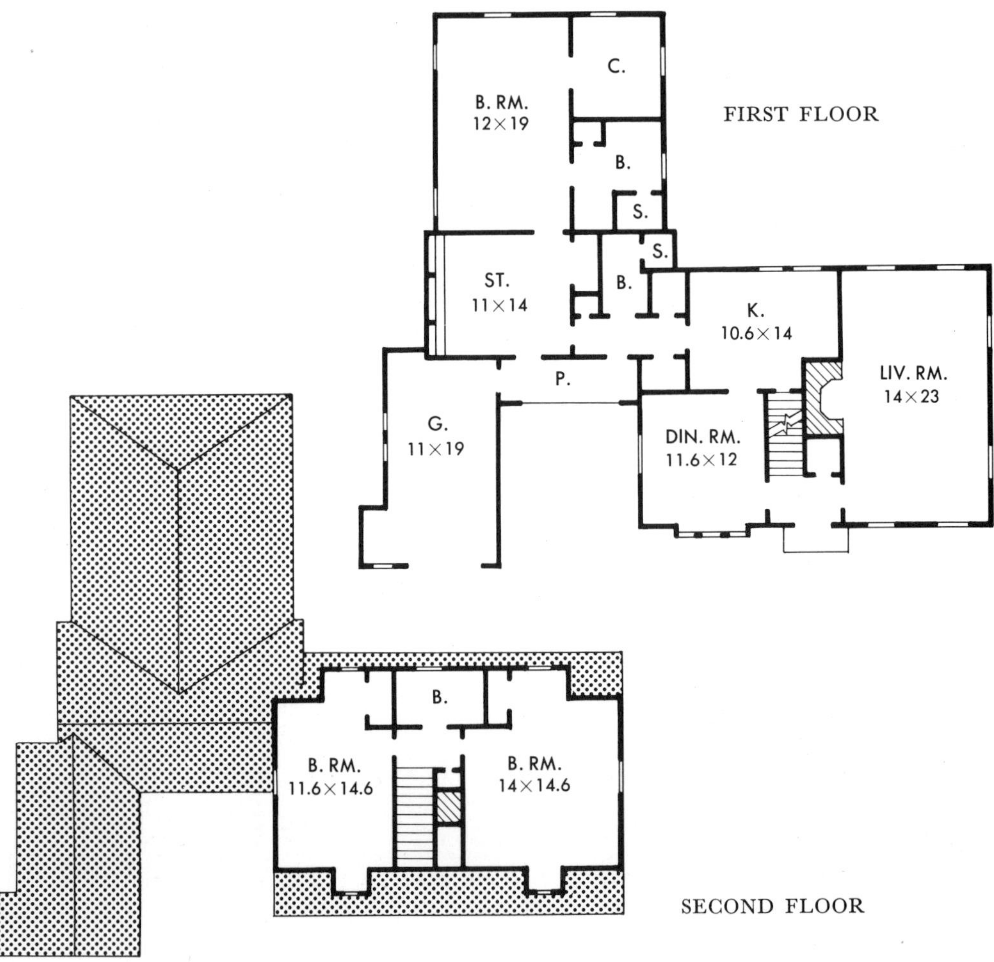

104. The Randall House (1952). Owner: Dr. R. V. Randall.

105. Randall House. Side view, showing distinctive details.

The Heck House

The streets sloped up on both sides of the corner lot that the Heck House was designed to fit. Houses are not always happy in such a situation, but this one manages it without difficulty (plates 106–108).

The detailing adds distinction to this house; note the small gable window, window brackets, birdhouse, and tiny fence (plate 106). The manner in which the bedroom wing is attached to the center section (plate 107) is also worth noting (see plan). An ordinary handling of the roof lines at this point would have been disastrous.

106. The Heck House (1949). Side view, showing bedroom wing. Owner: Mr. John Stroebel.

107. Heck House. Rear view, showing garage (left), porch, first- and second-floor bedrooms.

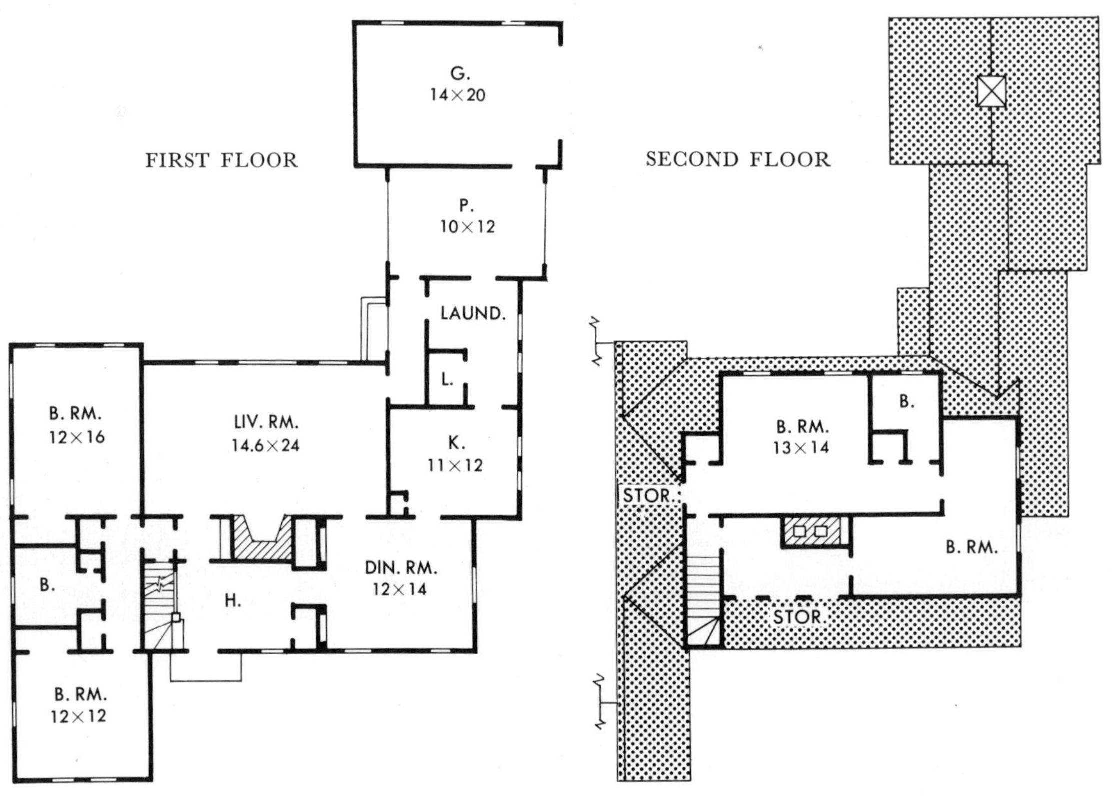

108. Heck House. Entrance, with bedroom wing (left).

⋆ *Old Cottages: Chimneys*

Unusually quaint, the little cottage with the eye-catching chimney (plate 109) was built about 1750. It originally rested on a foundation of timbers.

The flawless proportions of the Fowler House (plate 110) are properly crowned with a chimney of imperial size and excellence.

109. A diminutive cottage that grew (1750), East Sandwich, Mass.

110. The Fowler House (1720), Ipswich, Mass.

The Watson House

The Watson House (plate 111) is a modern version of the Cape Cod cottage. Its cheerful though unembellished appearance is the result of the almost perfect proportions of its masses, a provocative window treatment, and the carefully considered off-center balance (plate 112).

Houses of this type—and especially their main sections—must be purposely designed to look comparatively small from the front. Otherwise there is great danger that the finished product will appear clumsy and ill-proportioned. As with most of the others, the true size of the Watson House can be seen only from the rear (plate 113).

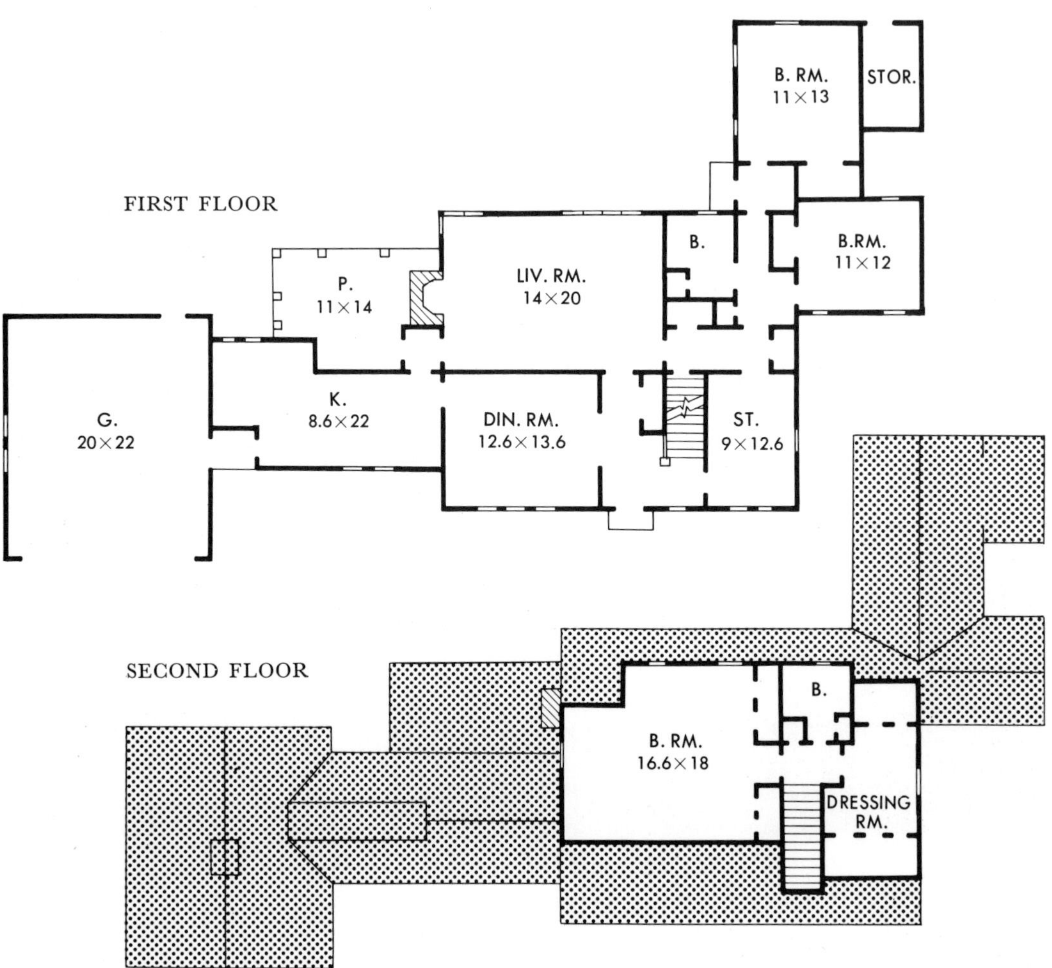

111. The Watson House (1957). Owner: Mr. Roy Watson.

112. Watson House. Front view, showing distinctive window treatment.

113. Watson House. Rear view.

The Moore Duplex

The duplex or double-house as usually seen on American streets can seldom be regarded as an asset to a neighborhood. But there is no excuse for the carelessness that almost invariably goes into its design. All of the traditional two-story types of houses are rich in qualities that can be adapted to this kind of dwelling, and there are few streets in the land to which a house like the Moore Duplex (plates 114, 115) would not be an acceptable addition. Note especially the fine entrance (plate 114), a modern continuance of the old traditions.

114. The Moore Duplex (1939). Entrance. Owner: Mr. Charles Hutchinson.

115. Moore Duplex.

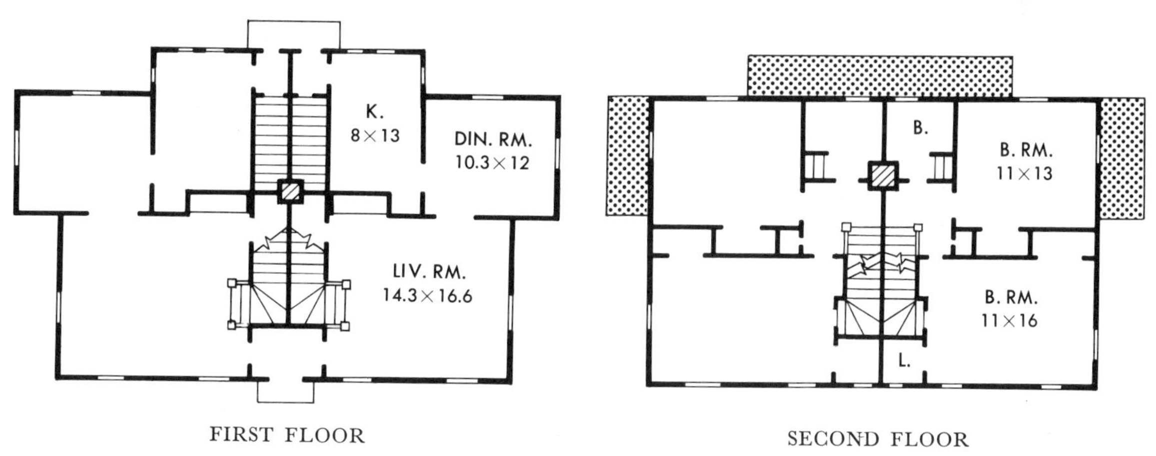

FIRST FLOOR

SECOND FLOOR

PART TWO

★ *A Massachusetts Mansion*

Developing from a humble beginning, the gambrel roof eventually crowned great houses that approached the apogee of elegance long before the War of the Revolution. The gambrel roof shown here (plate 117) graces a house built by Colonel Joseph Stebbins, a Revolutionary patriot, in 1772. At that time the village of Deerfield, Massachusetts had a minister named Ashley who was an outspoken Tory. Colonel Stebbins had strong feelings on the burning questions of the day, and he decidedly had scant time for Tories. So, when he was married, he refused to permit the controversial parson to officiate at his wedding. Instead, he loaded his prospective bride, Lucy Frary, into a buggy and took off for Hinsdale, New Hampshire, where he found a preacher more to his liking.

In the house Colonel Stebbins built for his bride, we can see how the influence of the Georgian style was making itself felt in New England architecture. Here are quoins and a modillioned cornice. Here are sensitively executed entrances whose perfectly proportioned pilasters have angular Ionic capitals. Here, in short, is Colonial excellence.

It was fortunate, indeed, that the Colonel had the foresight to build such a great and roomy mansion. He and Lucy had thirteen children.

116. The Stebbins Mansion (1772). Entrance. Old Deerfield, Mass.

117. Stebbins Mansion.

PART TWO

The Johnson House

The Johnson House (plate 118), with its unusual eye appeal, was for several years the author's home. In those days, before the growing trees and shrubbery began to conceal its lines, the house was tremendously photogenic from all angles. Almost every day, sightseers would stop to record its lovely image on film.

Plate 119 is a black-and-white version of a fine color photograph by Warren Reynolds; it was taken for an *American Home* magazine article titled "A Great American Classic." The house exemplifies the contemporary Cape Cod dwelling in its most popular form. It has all the touches that are, in the public mind, associated with the New England cottage. Breezeway and cupola, dentils and postlamps, fences and hedge—all are here in one carefully fashioned composition. It is crowned with a proud chimney which in turn is capped by four fat pots (plate 121).

For a house of this type and size, the pitch of the roof is unusually steep, rising twelve inches in a twelve-inch run. Since the house is twenty-eight feet in depth, a conventionally fashioned dormer would be heavy and clumsy in appearance. The dormer is hip-roofed, and the way it has been handled is worth study (plate 121).

When the issue of *American Home* featuring the Johnson House first appeared a few years ago, the public response was overwhelming. Within six weeks, more than 1,400 readers had ordered the sets of plans that *American Home* was distributing. It was an eloquent testimonial to the popularity of the Colonial dwelling—convincing proof that we have not seen the last of such houses.

118. The Johnson House (1946). Owner: Dr. W. J. Johnson.

119. Johnson House. Courtesy of Downe Publishing, Inc.

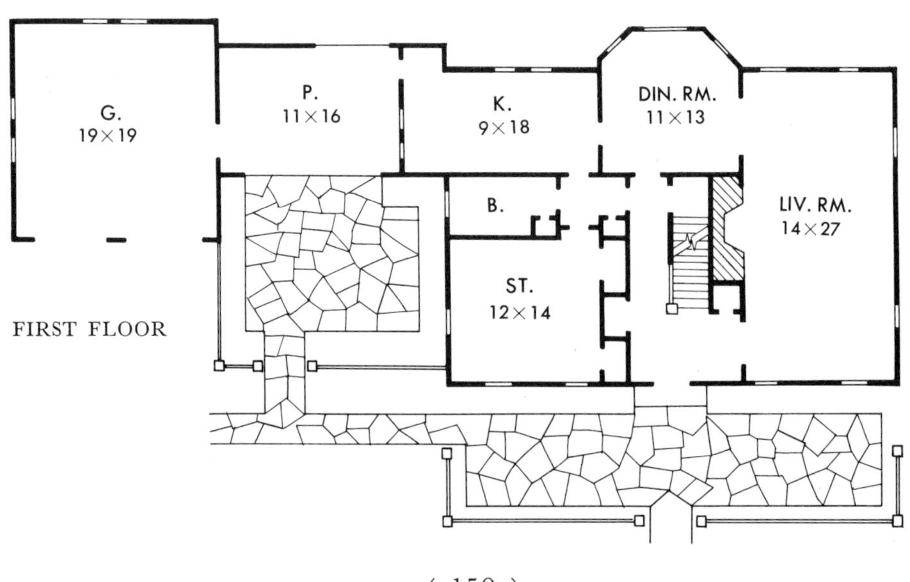

FIRST FLOOR

120. *Johnson House. Side view.*

SECOND FLOOR

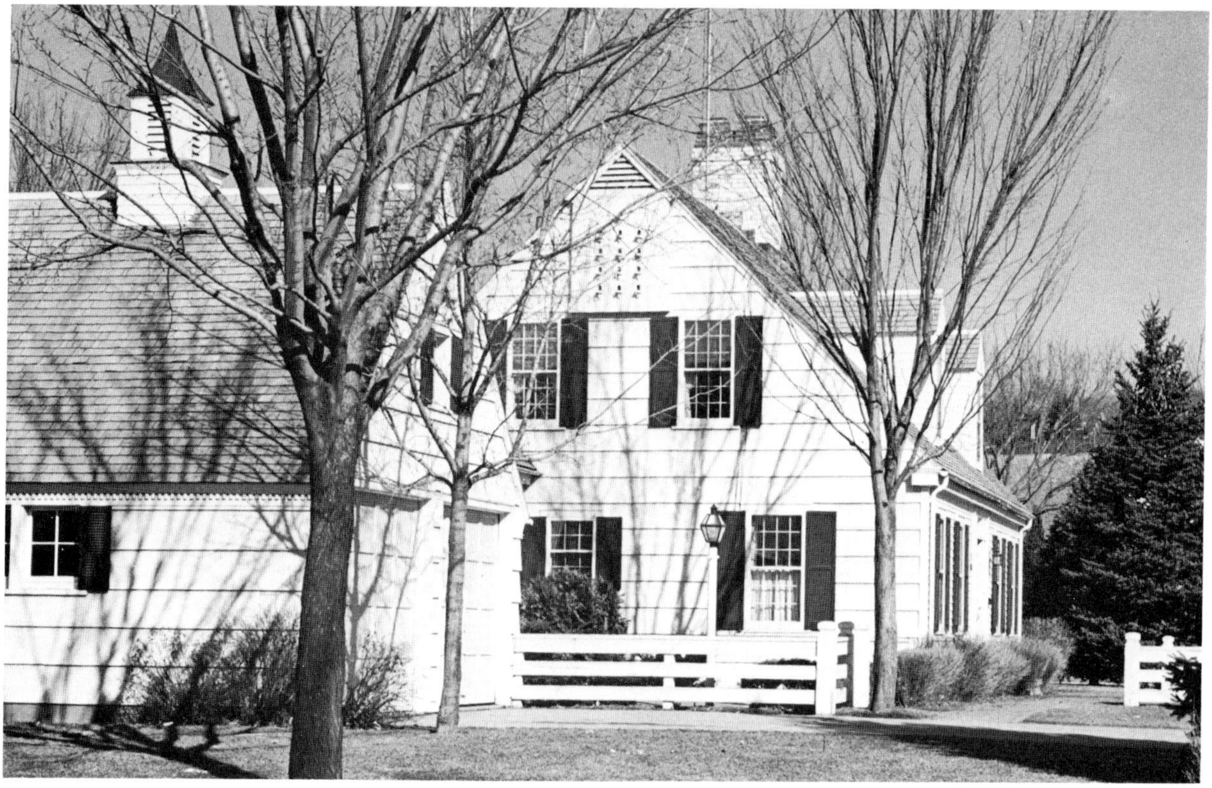

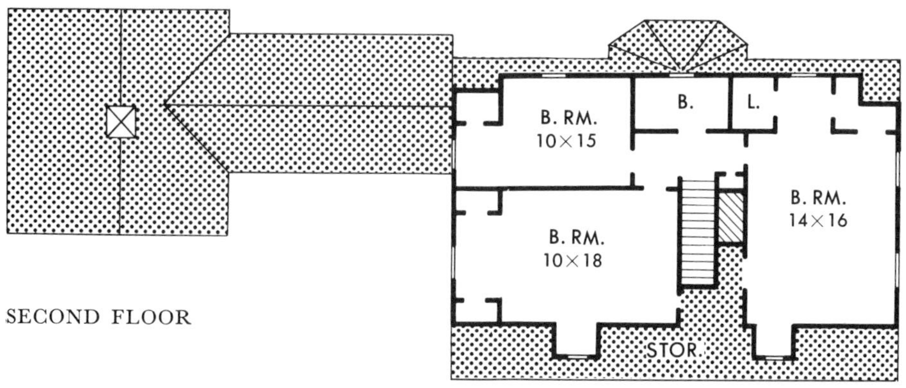

121. Johnson House. Rear view.

The Osborn House

Serene and simple, the Osborn House (plates 122–124) is in happy contrast to the caricatures often passed off as "Cape Cod."

The quiet dignity of this pitched-roof cottage (plate 122) is based on simplicity—the keynote to success in the design of such a house. From Sandwich to Provincetown the quiet streets on the Cape are dotted with its prototypes.

122. The Osborn House (1947). Owner: Mrs. J. E. Osborn.

The irregular floor plan of the Osborn House played an important part in the creation of an interesting exterior. And again a judicious combination of clapboards, shingles, and boards with battens has produced the desired result. The rambling appendages on this fine home (plate 123) interpret truly the spirit of Cape Cod.

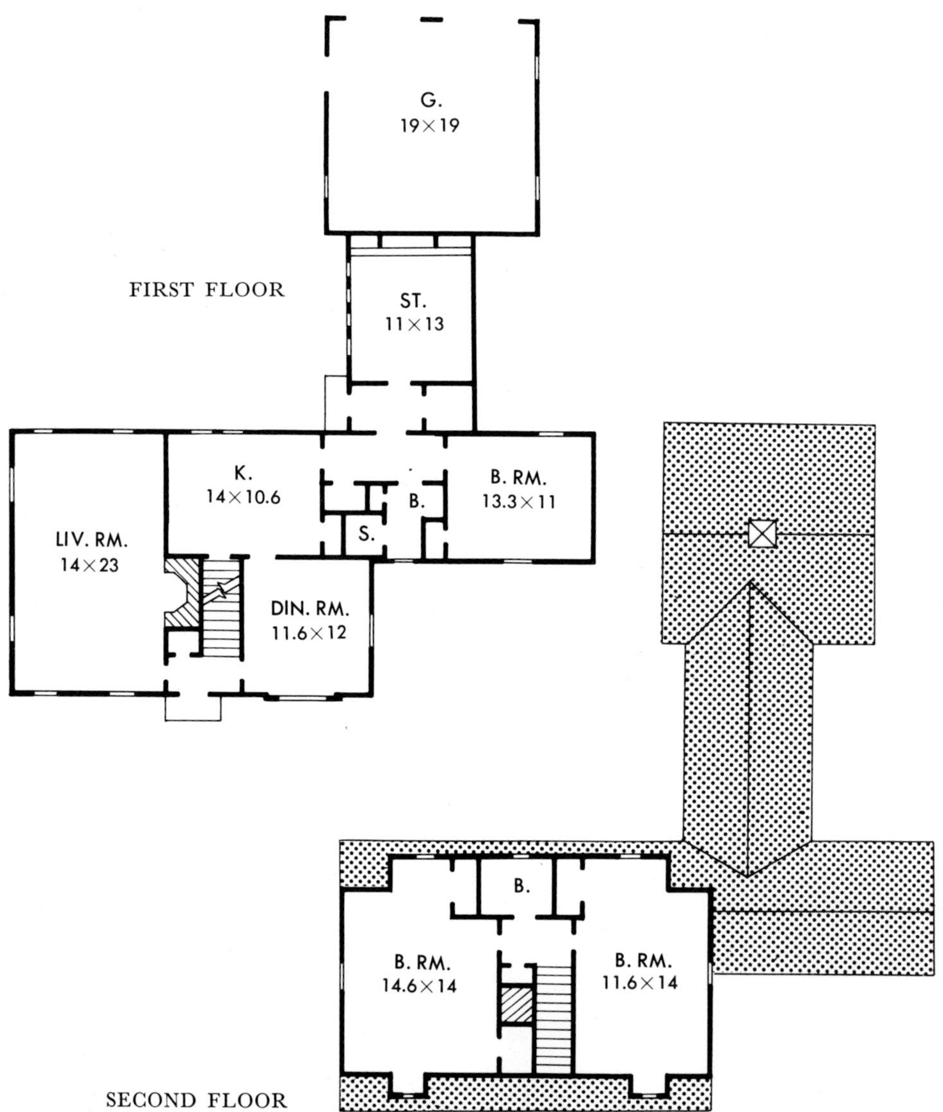

FIRST FLOOR

SECOND FLOOR

123. Osborn House. Exterior, showing rambling appendages.

124. Osborn House. Rear view.

PART TWO

★ *The Atwood and Dobyns Houses*

Pictured here (plates 125, 128) is the Atwood House, the oldest dwelling in Chatham, far out on the elbow of Cape Cod. Although the gambrel roof is not very common in Cape Cod houses, the example which graces the Atwood House is among the finest specimens in all New England. This venerable dwelling is now the home of the Chatham Historical Society, and history-minded readers will probably be interested to know that the remains of Squanto, the Indian who befriended the Pilgrims during the ordeal of their first winter, are buried somewhere near this very spot. He died in 1622, on the English sloop *Swan* as it lay at anchor in Stage Harbor, only a few steps from the site.

The Dobyns House (plate 126), another former home of the author, is an outstanding example of a gambrel-roof Cape Cod dwelling with many additions. A polished adaptation of the Atwood House, it was originally built to simulate a structure to which appendages had been added from time to time (plate 127). Later, two actual additions were built (plates 129–131). The first-floor plan (p. 159) shows the original house with dark lines and the kitchen and bedroom additions with lighter lines. With each addition, the appearance of the house grew more interesting; as the plans and photographs show, it is well worth close scrutiny and careful study.

Like its predecessor, the Dobyns House was obviously built to last and, despite its sophistication, it has much of the character so apparent in the Atwood House. This character is clearly visible in the new bedroom wing (plates 131, 132) as well as the gambrel roof (plate 133) and the rear of the finished house (plate 130). The tremendously interesting roof lines show up in the second-floor plan (p. 159). The broken lines are those of the later additions.

125. The Atwood House (1752), Chatham, Mass. Prototype of the Dobyns House.

126. The Dobyns House (1953). Owner: Dr. J. H. Dobyns.

127. Dobyns House. Front view.

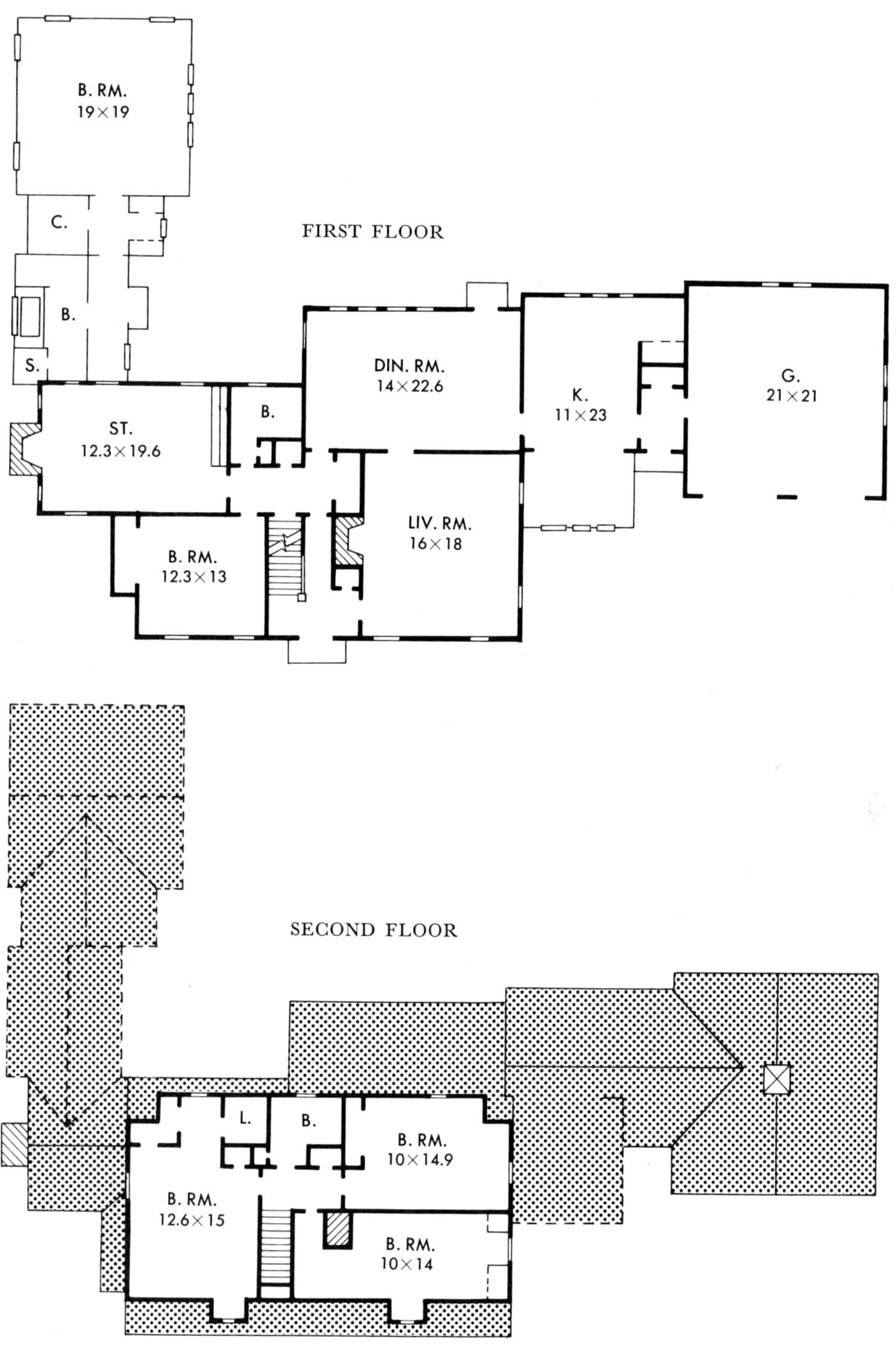

B. RM.
19×19
C.
B.
S.
FIRST FLOOR
DIN. RM.
14×22.6
K.
11×23
G.
21×21
ST.
12.3×19.6
B.
LIV. RM.
16×18
B. RM.
12.3×13
SECOND FLOOR
L.
B.
B. RM.
10×14.9
B. RM.
12.6×15
B. RM.
10×14

128. Atwood House. Rear view.

129. Dobyns House. Rear view, original structure, showing proportioning of "additions" to center section.

130. Dobyns House. Rear view.

131. Dobyns House. New bedroom wing.

132. Dobyns House. Closer view, bedroom wing.

133. Dobyns House. Perfect gambrel roof against a winter sky.

The interior views (plates 134–136) show the rooms as they appeared when this house was the home of the author. The woodwork in the sitting room was jewel-like blue, as in the parlor of the Stebbins Mansion in Old Deerfield; the sofa and lounge chair were covered in antique yellow leather; the rug was Oriental, in faded blues and reds; the furniture, mahogany.

134. Dobyns House. Living room.

135. Dobyns House. Dining room.

136. Dobyns House. "Blue Sitting Room."

Conclusion

THE QUALITIES that were the very essence of the old New England houses show no sign of exhaustion. These pages have presented pictorial evidence of how richly adaptable they are to the needs of present-day living. Through the camera eye we have seen that the Colonial forms of design are tremendously flexible. The high regard in which they have been held for three centuries should be convincing proof that they are supremely satisfying. The ancient concepts of design are sound and, even more important, they are mature. Fundamentally and aesthetically they meet every test; it is therefore beyond doubt that, unless some unforeseen and radical change occurs in our way of life, contemporary versions of the homes of our New England ancestors will continue to be built and will remain in high favor. They are not going to disappear on any near tomorrow, as the excited advocates of the various "new looks" in house design will eventually discover. And, as the picture on the following page testifies, traditional New England architecture is ageless in its simplicity and beauty.

Omne non est Gloria
. . . but with dignity unimpaired,
this ancient dwelling pays its toll to Time.

137. A New England relic.

Glossary

batten: a strip of wood used to fasten or cover seams between boards
bowed roof: a slightly curved roof
bracket: a support projecting from a wall; normally designed to hold a vertical load, but often serving merely as decoration
breezeway: a covered passageway, sometimes enclosed on the sides, connecting a house and a garage

capital: the top of a column or pilaster
casement: a hinged window frame that opens outward; often two frames meeting in the center of a window and opening out like French doors
chimney pot: a pipe set on the top of a chimney to carry smoke away and increase the draft
clapboard: a thin, narrow board with one edge thicker than the other, used for covering the outer walls of frame houses
Colonial Period: 1620–1780
cornice: a horizontal molding along the top of a wall, building, etc., or the upper molding projecting from a horizontal structure supported by columns
cupola: a small, domelike structure set on a roof

dentil: small, square blocks projecting like teeth, usually ornamenting a cornice
dormer: a roofed projection in which a window is set upright in a sloping roof
double-hung window: a window with a sash supported on each side by a counterweighted sash cord or a spring tension device for holding the sash in position, raising it, or lowering it

eaves: the lower border of a roof overhanging a wall
ell: an appendage set at a right angle to the main building

Federal Period: 1780–1820
fenestration: the arrangement of a building's windows and doors

gable roof: a ridged roof with sloping sides making triangular enclosures of the upper parts of a building's end walls
gambrel roof: a roof with two slopes on each side; the lower, steeper slope changes abruptly to a flatter slope continuing to the ridge
Georgian: the basically classical style characteristic of the reigns of George I, II, III, and IV of Great Britain (1714–1830)

half-house: a structure built as if it were only half of a house but serving as a complete dwelling; the floor plan allows for the other half to be added fairly simply
hip roof: a pyramidal roof with sloping eaves overhanging all four sides of a house

Ionic: having ornamental scrolls on the capitals

lean-to: a shed or appendage with the rafters of its one-sloped roof resting their upper ends against the wall of the main building

modillion: an ornamental block or bracket under a cornice

panel: a flat, usually rectangular piece of wood covering a wall, door, or other surface; sometimes it is framed, raised, recessed, or otherwise set off
parapet: a wall or railing functioning as a protection against falling
pediment: a decorative triangular structure, a low-pitched gable; usually on the front of a building or over a doorway
pilaster: a thin, flat, rectangular column set against a wall
pitched roof: a roof with sloping sides
portico: a porch or covered walk with a roof supported by columns

quoin: a large, rectangular stone used to tie the external corners of a building together or to decorate the corners of wooden buildings

salt-box house: a two-story house with a short roof pitch in front and a longer pitch in the rear, where a lean-to shed has been added
segmental: arched; having the form of a segment of a circle
shingles: thin, wedge-shaped boards laid in overlapping rows as roofing or siding